W9-DDI-134

THE ADVENTURE OF BEING YOU

By Robert James St. Clair:

NEUROTICS IN THE CHURCH

THE ADVENTURE OF BEING YOU

The Adventure of Being You

Robert James St. Clair

FLEMING H. REVELL COMPANY
WESTWOOD • NEW JERSEY

Unless otherwise identified, Scripture quotations are from *The Revised Standard Version of the Bible*, copyright 1946 and 1952.

On p. 17, the two quotations from *The Exploration of the Inner World*, by Anton Boisen, are reprinted by permission of the publisher, Harper & Row, Publishers, Inc.

The poem "A Plaint of Complexity" (pp. 26–27) is from *Body and Raiment* by Eunice Tietjens. Copyright 1919 by Alfred A. Knopf, Inc., and renewed 1947 by Cloyd Head. Reprinted by permission of Alfred A. Knopf, Inc.

The two quotations from *Time's* cover story on London, which appear on pp. 36 and 37, are from the April 15, 1966, issue of *Time*. They are reprinted here, courtesy *Time;* © Time Inc. 1966.

The selection on p. 62 from the Sydney J. Harris column is reprinted by permission of Sydney J. Harris and Publishers Newspaper Syndicate.

The poem "Thank God I'm Alive," on p. 77, is from *Hilltop Verses and Prayers*, by Ralph S. Cushman. Copyright 1945 by Whitmore and Stone (Abingdon Press). Used with permission of the publisher.

The poem "Word from the Prodigal," by C. Moore Hunt, on p. 79, is copyright 1964 Christian Century Foundation. Reprinted from the July 1, 1964, issue of *The Christian Century*, by permission of the author and the Foundation.

On p. 97, letters from Ann Landers column are reprinted by permission of Publishers Newspaper Syndicate.

The poem "I See His Blood Upon the Rose," which appears on p. 101, is from *The Collected Poems of Joseph Mary Plunkett;* reprinted with permission of the publishers, Talbot Press Ltd., Dublin.

The poem "Kind of an Ode to Duty" (pp. 116–117) is from *Verses from 1929 On*, by Ogden Nash, copyright 1935 by The Curtis Publishing Co. Reprinted by permission of Little, Brown and Co., Boston, and J. M. Dent & Sons Ltd., London.

The poem on p. 154 by Lona Fowler ("A Great Thought") is reprinted with permission of the author and *Concern* magazine; from the Feb., 1964, issue of *Concern*, official magazine of United Presbyterian Women.

• WESTWOOD, NEW JERSEY • LIBRARY OF CONGRESS CATALOG CARD NUMBER: 66-21897 • PRINTED IN THE UNITED STATES OF AMERICA • I.I

To
WILLIAM H. GATES,
Pastor of the Northminster United Presbyterian Church, Cincinnati, Ohio, my good friend since the days of our new lives in Christ,
and
CHARLES QUERRY,
Principal of Hyre Junior High School in Akron, Ohio, and Presbyterian elder, a man of patience, courage, and clear vision,
this book is dedicated with respect and affection.

Author's Preface

IF THE QUESTION should be asked, "Is this book about religion?"—and it certainly looks like a religious book—we would have to know which of the two kinds of religion you mean.

Do you mean the really sweet piety-in-the-sky type of religion? The fanfare in flowing robes, the hypnotism before candles, the morbid preoccupation with its own insides, the type earth-shaken by debate over altar guilt and tranquilized by visions of when the roll is called up yonder? The religion that reminds you of a stout woman in her first evening dress, standing for an hour before mirrors? Or of a fireman patiently examining the curious construction of the hose while the house is burning? The kind trapped by itself in itself? The kind whose power is in direct proportion to the popularity of the pastor, and whose worship offering is the incense of the church machine's burning gears? No. This book isn't about that kind of religion.

If you mean the other kind, yes. This is the kind, of course, that thinks about God interacting with people as they are. Whatever God may be apart from human life, what He does with His "time," and whatever He may be doing in the heavens on other planets, we don't know. But we know He created this life, and that He is at work in life and is re-creating it to the satisfactions of its original purpose. Yes, this is the kind of religion we mean.

God shows Himself in the stuff of life. He did it in the life of Christ, and we know this because we knew He had been doing it in all other lives. Empathy with and the study of human beings and their condition are just as important for theology as the study of the Bible. In fact, lacking openness to self and awareness of other persons, you can't begin to understand the Bible. You can study Greek and match verses and become a religious egocentric and a pious detriment to the happiness of everyone else. More and more I get increasingly nervous in the presence of overly religious people—whatever is bugging them soons starts bugging me.

Except for those who were divorced from life, people usually felt quite comfortable in Jesus' presence. It was not His miraculous power, but His being a genuine Man, which got Him in bad with the Pharisees. It was His love for life which alienated organized religion and got Him killed.

But when we speak of "real life," we don't necessarily mean the world "in the raw." Life at its worst is quite evident. What is life at its best? What does this "best" mean for the golden universal man, and for any one man of flesh and blood?

Beneath the horror of sin, what is the truth to decipher about man as he was meant to live? And out of the raw materials of his tears and smiles, dreams and heartaches, how can he construct a life that has no argument with life, a venture that vindicates itself in the open secret of its own joy?

These are good religious questions. I have a standing debate with a psychologist who insists that materialistic science can show the way and provide the tools. Who needs God? All I say to him is that the religious life is not simply one of bravely wiping away the tears and getting adjusted. It is not the performance of cold-eyed, systematic altruism. It is living an inspired faith in what Christ reveals of life in us. It may reveal more obstacles than psychology can remove, it may bring us to weaknesses and strife that will never be removed—in ourselves and in the world—and cause us to die trying. It may leave us with a sickening sense of being shortchanged in view of what could have been accomplished. This is faith that will not let us go. It is a trust that keeps us afloat when by all obvious standards, although we appeared good and busy, we felt ourselves to be sinking.

By faith we are grateful. Through faith we worship God as we are, as the world is.

This faith is a gift, but a gift we cannot *live* without. It is a gift given by the Creator to the created in full view of a running succession of disasters in the creation.

No one, therefore, can be on good terms with the fullest life who is not on good terms with God, and those who trust God are trusting life. That is what this book is all about.

Contents

THE ADVENTURE OF BEING YOU

1

The Creation of Life

THE LIVING OF life in the fullest adventure is the will of God. Pierre Ceresole said, "All these somberly moral people whose characteristic is renunciation completely forget what is essential. It is not morality, however indispensable and respectable that is. . . . The essential is the joy, the splendor, the magnificence of each man, of all men. Virtue is only a means. The essential is life—splendid life. There is no greater mistake than to imagine the Eternal looking with a pleased smile at these pale little virtues. What the Eternal loves is life—beautiful, powerful, intense—and everything which can strengthen it, make it last in the world, strong and active."

Modern science is today, more than ever before, studying the nature and origin of life itself. The most adventuresome of philosophers are searching for a unitary principle underlying all creation, a Life that co-inheres in all life, an all dominating Life *above*—yet *in*—all sub-systems of life, organic and inorganic.

Men have always, to be sure, sought the unity of life. The adventures of the whole man living to the full are daring, breathtaking, filled with the spell of the million-orbed gleams of truth from every facet of every soul. To be a whole man is to be on intimate terms with all living men, and to feel a kinship with all that exists.

Emerson said, "For the sense of being which in calm hours rises, we know not how, in the soul, is not diverse from things, from space, from light, from time, from man, but one with them and proceeds obviously from the same source whence their life and being also proceed."

According to the Bible, in Galatians 5:22, when persons are possessed by the sacred Spirit of life, they possess love, joy, peace, each denoting the unity experienced with oursives, with others, with creation.

In his book *Religions, Values and Peak-Experiences*, Abraham H. Maslow, psychologist at Brandeis University, makes known to us the results of scientific analysis of our peak-experiences. These are the transcendent events similar to the high point of conversion, or the mountain-top experience of the prophet. Dr. Maslow says these experiences are not distinctly religious or weird. They are universal, belonging to men of every age and clime. He says that in these experiences the cosmos is perceived as a unified whole. There is tremendous concentration, and things and persons are perceived as more detached from human concerns. The perceiver can regard nature in its own right without demanding people or things conform (to what I shall later call the "microcosm," the private world of the constricted man).

Dr. Maslow goes on to say that in these experiences, perception is ego-transcending, unselfish. They give meaning to life, and it proves that there are supremely worthy goals in life. Universality and eternity are experienced, and time seems to stand still. The one experiencing may lose the sense of time and matter.

Dr. Maslow says the most important finding is that there are basically intrinsic values, eternal verities—the spiritual values. Things and people can be sacred. There is general agreement on what is supremely beautiful and of ultimate value. Naturally, emotions of awe, wonder, and worship are evoked. Persons in such a state feel grateful, deeply blessed, as the Apostle Paul felt in his moments of sublime revelation.

The Jews did not simply broadcast near and far that there was the Creative Life responsible for both dust and the man related to dust; they called this Life "God," and named Him, and His attributes, and personality. The Psalmist linked heaven and earth, flesh and spirit, man and creation, and the prophets knew that when full redemption occurred, both man and beast would live in harmony. Paul and the writer of Revelation stated with Jesus that the religious struggle on earth is a cosmic one, and all creation will one day be summed up in the rule of God in Christ.

We are beginning to feel now that all things have lives of their own, a fact certainly more acceptable since Newtonian physics declined in favor of Quantum physics and indeterminateness. Charles Hartshorne, in his book *Reality as Social Process*, states, "The social theory of existence denies that any individual unit of reality (excluding mere composities from the class of 'unit') is absolutely without feeling or free creative action." Every being has psychic, free or creative, relative, and temporal aspects. God is the all-dominating Being related to all sub-systems and beings, and coordinates all activities into a world order.

Well, if this is true, then you can just imagine what this would mean down through the ages for men with an eye clear to true being, and a hunger for God! Knowledge of God is actually experience! Being is unity with this God, and Deity can be perceived fully in man. But which man?

The theme of the present book is found in John 1: "In the beginning was the Word, and the Word was with God, and the Word was God. He was in the beginning with God; all things were made through him, and without him was not anything made that was made. In him was life, and the life was the light of men" (JOHN 1:1–4).

Not only John, but Paul, and the writer of Hebrews also, state that all things were made through Christ. Christian theology has failed to come to grips with this fact. Is it a symbolic exaggeration? Is it literally true? How are we to understand it? And what is the relation between creation through Christ and redemption by Christ? What are the characteristics of the life flowing from, and drawn back to, God as we know Him in Christ? What does the true nature of man tell us of the nature of God, and what does the nature of God in Christ tell us about the true nature of man?

Unfortunately, it is possible—no! *prevalent*, for men the creators to remake their own world, scaled down to their own dimensions in order to build a fence around anxiety and hold it in. This small world we call "the microworld." This is an allegedly static, discrete system which exists primarily in imagination, although in externals it may coincide with a family, a club, a church, or even a nation. It is a group of persons associated by a common devotion to a fetish, a core artificial value such as status, license, superiority, or even "love." On the basis of the scheme of things in this little world, men structure their relations and learn how to subdue others by blackmail, flattery, a common devotion, and mutual support of a kind.

The net effect of living in one or more microworlds is to militate against the eternal life. Eventually, a pane of glass ever so thin stands between the constricted man and those "over there," especially you and you, whoever you are. People become mixers who mingle but rarely love. Life is expected to open automatically, and souls are searched out who promise to believe what we tell them about ourselves. Soon the glass grows yellow with age and caked with dirt. The "protected" man cannot see too well out there, and they "out there" cannot see in. Well, what matter! As they say, "Better to be safe than sorry."

The great pain of living comes to those whose chief goal is the avoidance of the pains of broken love, disappointments, rejection, and social crucifixion. This death is the exchange of reality for illusion, one's life for a fetish, the glory of God for the imagined glories of man—pride.

We are first condemned because the Creator will not be satisfied with our little joy, our small confidence, our weak love, our tentative self-realization, and our limited perception of truth and beauty. To believe, we must be given to the fullness of the Creator, and we require forgiveness for not experiencing the fullness of life. Out of our conflicts we come to God, only to discover that we have the power to live in a new tension. Christian belief is a comforting dissatisfaction, a motivating agitation, a conquering inability, and a peacemaking disturbance.

When we call repeated attention in this book to Christ as Agent and End of creation, . . . "all things were created through him . . ." (COLOSSIANS 1:16)—we are stating that the divine life of the Creator was destined by His will inherent in creation to be imparted through the Spirit of Christ, and without the full union of the Spirit of life in Christ (ROMANS 8:2) with our lives, the full purpose of creation could never come to pass.

The immediate purpose of God in Christ was to forgive sin. The ultimate purpose was to vindicate His own sovereign life by completing His creation of man. Francis W. Beare states, "The 'living soul' imparted to man at the creation required to be supplemented by the 'life-giving spirit' of the Redeemer (I COR. 15:45–49). A great vista of theological speculation is opened here, which has been explored only sporadically."

Christ continues God's work of redemption-creation through His Spirit, the Spirit of life fully at home and at one with the spirit of all men. Anton T. Boisen, founding spirit of the Clinical Pastoral Training Movement, who thought and wrote fifty years ahead of his time, said, "Face to face with the impending destruction of the national life and of the national hope, the divine spirit of the race which was focused in him gave up its life and became thereby the Divine Spirit of the world." In his mental illness Boisen often lived in some tortured form of a peak-experience. He states, "During all that period the idea of some great Earth Spirit or some Solar Spirit was present. The exact character of this Spirit was not clear but its high destiny lay in Christ, in whom all the finest possibilities centered."

As for me, the more I study the "self-actualizing person" of the dynamic-holistic school of psychology (Kurt Goldstein and Abraham Maslow), and the holistic school of psychiatry (Karen Horney and Andras Angyal), and the "fully functioning person" described by Carl Rogers, the more I am inclined to yield myself to the Spirit of Christ. I believe that in Clinical Pastoral Education growing and enthusiastic attention will be devoted to the person and operation of the Holy Spirit.

Those who wish to explore the effectuation of authentic selfhood in Christ will profitably use *Christ and Selfhood*, by Wayne Oates. The unity of mind and body is being discussed in most intriguing fashion by Ludwig von Bertalanffy. It is recommended that the reader remember the unity of knowledge and being in the matter of ultimate verities of the Spirit, and that personal study of the Scriptures and prayer will be the most valuable means of ascending to peak-experiences. An excellent devotional book I return to time and again is *Abundant Living*, by E. Stanley Jones.

Our hearts ache as we survey the intolerable shame and

tragedy which are the existence of so many souls. And yet we cannot ignore the truth of the marvelous works of the Spirit of Christ in man's heart. Intimations of the renewal and eternalness of life are everywhere. It is the Spirit of Christ who can lead us from failure and death to the very source of life. Those who embrace Him flee to life. Then we know that the love of God has overcome all separations. The last sigh must be laughter, the last comment singing!

We are bound to give thanks for our destiny—the victory of life.

2

My Self, Come Forth!

I NOTICE THESE days that many forces are urging us to change. In the movies we are persuaded to get more out of life by "getting away from it all," and on TV we are asked if we wouldn't like to become blondes in order to have more fun. There are so many ways to help us be something or someone else that anyone who is contented with himself might be considered retarded or conceited. Who would you like to be?

Have you ever wondered who the "you" we're talking about really is, and whether or not you'd recognize the real you if you met him on the street? Have you ever had the urge to stand before an audience of some kind and shout, "Will the real *you* please stand up"?

I'm not sure that a lot that goes under the name of "religion" has had too much interest in this furtive fellow called "the real you." The New and Old Testaments used different language than we use, and the fact that we have good translations does not mean we possess accurate meanings. For example, a New Testament phrase is taken out of context, and the first thing you know someone is telling you that if you have self-esteem you are conceited, and that's bad. And unless you destroy the "old self," you are sinful. If you ask what the "old self" is, the answer comes back, "Maybe it's the ego."

The "ego"? What's that? To many it means one's pride or arrogance. If one has a strong ego, he must be haughty. That's bad, too.

Confused? Hop aboard! So are the rest of us.

Before we go further, let's say what we mean. The *self* is the image you hold of your total personality. It is an appraisal of you in all the roles you assume. It is a system of ideas about you as good or bad, great or insignificant, loved or unloved, and a combination of these in conflict. The self is your treasure. It is the value which determines how you think and feel before others. It is the *you.* It comes into being as a "self-system," which one psychiatrist defines as "an organization of educative experience called into being by the necessity to avoid or to minimize incidents of anxiety" (Harry Stack Sullivan).

There is no way to stop being a self. When some pious soul deplores the word "self" and—completely misunderstanding Christ—avers that we ought to burn the self, get rid of it, toss it into limbo somehow, he is inviting us to become some type of ghoul. How can a person stop being a person? If you were to find a way of destroying the self, you would be eliminating a human being.

The difficulty is partially caused by the thoughtless tossing about of words, and to many people "ego" means "self." Ego is then associated with such obscenities as "egocentered" and "egocentricity." What does the word mean for us here.

Where decisions are called for, the "ego" is that aspect of personality which makes adjustments to the world in order to satisfy inner needs.

The ego is told by the self how things really are and what values must be preserved in the interests of the self-image. The ego has memory, it has experience, it thinks, and it acts. It is driven by the need to deal with emotion, satisfy basic instinctive needs, and allay anxiety. And so it makes solutions, proceeds to do what is necessary, and directs, and restricts one's behavior. The methods of the ego change. Occasionally defensive mechanisms (like compensation, rationalization, etc.) are resorted to. The ego always looks to the future. It plans, thinks ahead, and never wants to be caught off guard. It must see that all parts of the personality operate as a whole, and that inner and outer conflicts are reconciled. When the ego can't do this, the person has a "nervous breakdown." He says this is "from overwork," but we know better, don't we?

In the present book no distinction is made between "body" and "spirit," simply because no distinction will hold up. The whole organism is the "soul"—the "body-self."

The self can and does change, because it is always being influenced. The self adopts the ideas it can live with safely and by which it judges its own worth. Father says: "Idle hands get into mischief, and the devil has you if you are wasting time"; or "You get into trouble easier than any boy I've ever seen." And so on. The emerging self hears these words, and its real religion comes into being.

The self can appreciate its abilities, think well of its background, and can exude self-esteem. The individual absorbs into himself the ideas and ideals with which he identifies himself. The self includes extensions of the self—things like an appropriate occupation, a good bank account, children who get A grades, a Cadillac, and whatever else is part of *you*. And the self can find itself so loathsome that the individual rejects himself as worthless. He may find the world so harsh and threatening that he bores into himself.

This "boring into one's self" produces a "constricted" person, who is a prisoner of his *microworlds*. I use this word to mean the tight little world of persons and ideas which he lives in with a minimum of anxiety and a maximum of support and appreciation. For example, in women you find that all the events and ideas about the child often become a microworld. The child gets married, and the destitute mother forces her husband to pack up and move across the country to become semiprofessional baby-sitters for the grandchildren.

This microworld has limits, defined by what is called "selective inattention" (Sullivan). Large spheres of experience and areas of the real world are closed off from view. The constricted person is not unconscious of them, but he becomes increasingly insensitive to them. Here, for example, is a man who has no time for Scouts, children's play, family activities, art, or other social experiences. He bores into the microworld of his work, and his job produces the "self-made man." He knows the self from the appraisals of his work, the comments of his boss, his pay raises, and his company awards. He ignores the comments of those who observe this selective inattention and remark that he is "in a rut." His microworld provides his true religion, and when he retires he is so desperately lost, constricted, and lonely that he falls to pieces.

Throughout this book we use the word "fetish." Use of the

word "idol" has been avoided because it has a certain connotation for me in my understanding of the neurotic personality. The "idol" of the neurotic is an all-pervading image of the self crystallized in a grandiose search for glory, which so typifies the neurotic personality. This image stresses quality, as, for example, the image of a super-intellect with expansive-vindictive trends who is right and brilliantly so in every situation he encounters.

The word "fetish," however, is more appropriate to the constricted personality, who is not necessarily bound by severe neurotic trends. It is an obsessive role, an embodiment of value in the microworld, with a defined set of ideas and pattern of behavior. The fetish may be simple or complex. It may be the role of any set pattern—outstanding sportsman, dedicated teacher, "absolutely free" and fun-loving bachelor, selfless politician, etc. It is compulsive and all-consuming, and becomes indistinguishable from the self. The fetish seems to become the self. There may be several fetishes to the one person. The fetish is not necessarily superior in quality to other roles and fetishes, but it is clung to because it is distinctly and utterly one's own. This element of pride places more and more of the real world into oblivion, so that the "death process" the Bible speaks of so much forces the constricted person into a deeper and deeper rut. And because it is one's own, it is essentially self-vindicating and "right." As the Biblical writers were so fond of reminding us, the outstanding feature of the constricted personality is his proud sense of self-righteousness.

When the self has become so artificial that it is in conflict with reality, with the real world, and when its principal devotion is to a restrictive fetish, then we are in trouble. What do we observe?

(*A*) We observe hampering inconsistencies. Ideals are thought to be performance. He's great because he is the best ________________(fill in the blank) in the________________, and those who doubt it are enemies, insensitive, callous, blind. But in other situations outside of the microworld he couldn't care less about his position. Mr. J. prays loud and long in the board of trustees. He is a real great prayer. Amen. But he doesn't care to pray for the family next door, because "they brought their troubles on themselves." That could be, too, but we observe here that Mr. J., great prayer, has a self which comes into its own only under certain restricted circumstances. Mr. J. is considered religious. But he may be constricted. Don't tell him. He wouldn't like it. His ego would have to go into action.

(*B*) His suspicions about the self are flippantly banished to oblivion. It becomes a matter of great pride to preserve the integrity of his freedom, ability to choose, decide, and think for himself.

Out of the night that covers me,
    Black as the pit from pole to pole,
I thank whatever gods may be
    For my unconquerable soul.

In the fell clutch of circumstance
    I have not winced nor cried aloud.
Under the bludgeonings of chance
    My head is bloody, but unbowed.

Beyond this place of wrath and tears
    Looms but the Horror of the shade,
And yet the menace of the years
    Finds, and shall find, me unafraid.

It matters not how strait the gate,
    How charged with punishments the scroll,
I am the master of my fate,
    I am the captain of my soul.

—William Ernest Henley

The selfish man stamps his feet firmly, but is like a mere flea on the tail of a large furry mongrel called "modern society"; and he cries, "I'm top dog around here!" Here is the forty-year-old adolescent who proclaims every day Independence Day, while secretly looking for a substitute parent to lean on or an enticing hole to crawl into.

(*C*) Sensitivity—now this is something to be reckoned with! It is an argument with his neighbors that they do not fit in with the preconceived image or plans of his self. Husbands with doubts about their manhood need to be assured by an admiring and adored goddess. So out of the blue sky they charge home and rake their poor wives over the coals for not being beautiful or for keeping an untidy home. But again, the selfish man is not quite sure what to think of others because he does not know what to think of himself. If his facade isn't flattered, he will go where he is appreciated.

(*D*) Numbness is inescapable. Spice becomes the variety of life. Pure sensation becomes the method of unifying the divided spirit and broken heart. The Psalmist prayed, "Teach me thy way, O Lord, that I may walk in thy truth; unite my heart to fear thy name" (PSALM 86:11). The constricted man prays, "Send me out to some foreign place, O Lord, where amidst the hogs I can buy a whole new image of myself." Sex, liquor, the party merry-go-round, and joy unconfined in the penny arcade—all four great pursuits patch up the icon's fragments with glue no stronger than the foam of sparkling zest. Unfortunately, the hangover's guilt only further depersonalizes and subdivides the battered self. What else is there to do but get lost in the neon jungle the next night and try a little harder? And a little harder. And a lit. . . .

(*E*) Disillusionment is for dessert. The ego becomes plainly confused because semiannually the self perceives some new pot of gold under the rainbow and strikes off after it with eyes lighted and heart pounding. Dedication to some new hobby or interest is unreserved. The husband gets a transfer to a new job and throws himself into it fourteen hours a day. Enthusiasm fades like a streaking comet. Each new venture is baptized with exhilaration and buried in disgust.

We are materialistic, all right. When you can't be sure about the value of self, you've got to buttress pride with the solid feel of things. Money you can count on. You can see it, feel it, look at its value printed right there, and store it away for future crises. On the one end of the spectrum is the fellow who is as safe as his bank account. At the other is the one who is prone to gambling and speculation. Both would like to bribe themselves into feeling safely loved.

(*F*) Because of fetishness, the constricted person loses the value, identity, and growth potential of the self. And once the self concept becomes fuzzy, he cannot adequately establish rapport with the life of all lives, the spirit of all selves.

One excellent study speaks of the "self concept," the nucleus, the central value relating to the self. When this core relates high morality with genuine self-esteem, the ego is able to function with efficiency and productivity. The more the self is truly able to think highly of itself and relate ego functions to the needs and emotions of others, the more the person is able to help others live their lives as they see fit without demanding that others bring life to him on his terms. When the self has a negative self image, our ego functions are sidetracked into mechanisms for safety, such as the grabbing of affection and the bribing of those who are reluctant to adore our fetishes. Hence we have the notion that it is one's self which gets in the way and ought to be dealt with ruthlessly, which is like saying that if a person gets sick too often we ought to exterminate him. As it is, if the self is beaten badly enough, the ego will devote its energies to artificial and power-wasting gimmicks to make up for the inner vacuum within the self.

The attention of the ego to the sculpturing of a fetish is the devotion to pride. And pride seeks to restore soundness and health to the self by the establishment of a reputation to this effect. (See I TIMOTHY 3:6 (*KJV*), where the Greek word for "being proud" is *tuphŏō*, meaning "to send up a smoke screen"; to envelop one's self with concealing smoke.) Pride is a cynical pronouncement of integrity. It is an open declaration of desperation that one is going to be faithful to the self no matter what the nagging doubts may whisper, as when the constricted man declares from the mountaintop, "My life may not be much, but by heaven it is *my* life; I made my bed and I shall lie in it." But here again, the reality of heaven and hell are inscribed on the atoms. As the years wear away, the question becomes, "What and where is the self with which I am supposed to be so intently preoccupied?"

Quite plainly, the ego may work itself to death (and you can take that phrase any way you want to) patching up numerous selves, each one of which is assumed to serve a valuable function. But not knowing which one is the real *me* isolates me from my powers, my destiny, and from the self of all selves, the life of all lives. This isolation prevents me from being an individual, and prevents me from seeing others as individuals. Righteousness becomes artificial or a decadent thing, and love degenerates into sticky goodness with a hidden ax to grind. And all the while any one of the acting selves may appear most appropriate and even—heaven help us!—self-effacing.

A Plaint of Complexity

I have too many selves to know the one.
In too complex a schooling was I bred,
Child of too many cities, who have gone
Down all bright cross-roads of the world's desires,
And at too many altars bowed my head
To light too many fires.

One polished self I have, she who can sit
Familiarly at tea with the marquise
And play the exquisite
In silken rustle lined with etiquette,
Chatting in French, Italian, what you please,
Of this and that—

And I've a modern, rather mannish self,
Lives gladly in Chicago.
She believes
That woman should come down from off her shelf
Of calm dependence on the male
And labor for her living.
She likes men,
And equal comradeship, and giving
As much as she receives.

I've a self compound of strange, wild things—
Of solititude, and mud, and savagery;
Loves mountain-tops, and deserts,
And the wings
Of great hawks beating black against the sky.

I've a self might almost be a nun,
So she loves peace, prim gardens in the sun
Where shadows sift at evening,
Hands at rest,
And the clear lack of questions in her breast.

And deeper yet there is my mother self,
Something not so much I as womankind,
That surges upward from a blind
Immeasurable past.

The best I am, or can be
This self stands
When others come and go, and in her hands
Are balm for wounds and quiet for distractions,
And she's the deepest source of all my actions.

But I've another self she does not touch,
A self I live in much, and overmuch
These latter years.
A self who stands apart from outward things,
From pleasure and from tears,
And all the little things I say and do.
She feels that action traps her, and she swings
Sheer out of life sometimes, and loses sense
Of boundaries and of impotence.

But what she sees in her far spirit world,
Or what the center is
Of all this whirl of crowding I's,
I cannot tell you—only this
That I've known too many selves to know the one.

—Eunice Tietjens

Jesus' command to deny the self does not mean drafting all selves into the military formations of a religious army or into the tight, superimposed regulations of a New Year's Day self-improvement binge. To the constricted man the command is a threat. It means—and should mean—that the fetishes ought to be burned because they are fetishes; and that the heathen in Africa and the pagans on Park Avenue don't want to because they can't, and can't because they don't want to. In the same way, the Ten Commandments were given as a threat to idols and a revelation of the holy nature of the universal spirit of divinely imparted life. At first glance God looks hostile.

While religion seems to concentrate too much about sin, the essential failure of religion has been to underestimate the consequences of sin, thus failing to call for what Christ demanded —namely, a radical adjustment of nothing less than the self. Most theology has been so engrossed in argument that the new emphasis is on the formulation of new ego skills. But, as already mentioned, the functioning of the ego depends on the self concept. What is needed is a theology dealing realistically with the radical change of the self. But this is precisely the point at which theology has met its Waterloo, and is only too happy to relinquish the field to a religious scheme of activism. Consequently, the American churches are extremely active atoning for individual guilt.

The radical change in the self must overcome the barrier of pride. "How can I fully be myself if I surrender fully to something or someone else? How can I lose my life and find it at one and the same time? How can I be me and not me? How can I find my individual, realized self if I am completely immersed in God?"

To answer these questions demands a long, hard look at Christ, and a long, hard look at one's self.

A study of the self impresses us with the indissoluble link between creation and redemption. Our knowledge of the self is rooted in the scientific facts available, what we know of ourselves, and in the incarnation of the Spirit of life in its maturity and perfection—Jesus Christ. The failures of humanity are fully gauged by contrasting the perfect maturity of manhood, as seen in Christ and which is available through the re-creative power of His Spirit, with our present alienation from both the Creator and our true, self-confident nature.

Our alienation from our selves means also our estrangement from the self of all selves, the soul of all men, the spirit of all life created by the one God. For a soul to be successful in fetish worship by thoroughly believing in the power of his own gods, he would have to become a complete stranger to the emerging selves of his neighbors and from the one life of love, hope, peace, and joy which is potentially in all and through all. If he is enabled to return to himself, however, it must be through the creative power of this Spirit of life, which restores him to the true life of all men. The constricted man may surrender himself in sexual love and feel at one with lovers everywhere. This feeling is so potent that the Apostle Paul uses it as a special illustration of the relationship of Christ to the church. Likewise, this same man may surrender himself to events of great joy, hope, and peace, and experience this same transcendent self-realization. Life is one. But without the indwelling Spirit of life being active and ascendent in the individual spirit, man is temporarily and tentatively saved. He stands on the threshold of true salvation. He runs the risk of exploiting the very facet of life which might have brought him over the threshold to the life of God.

Christ threatens our fetishes by His humanity, identifies the Spirit of life, and now comes to us as this very Spirit.

Revealing the Spirit of all creation, through His suffering death and triumphant resurrection, He now calls this Spirit the "Spirit of grace." This same Christ is Universal Man, the forerunner of the true race of men, immersed in our battles, temptations, dreary routines, and wearying tasks. He alone knows in Himself the depth of man's fall from the glory of God's life, which he should have shared and from which he took flight. Christ's life is the life which God shares with us.

It is possible for men to be caught by the wonder and beauty of the true life. They can take full responsibility for the sufferings inflicted on Christ, look at their fetishes realistically, and ask the Spirit of grace to destroy forever the barriers between themselves and the life eternal.

It seems that Christ's sufferings were senseless. Who hath believed our report? We report that the Way, the Truth, and the Life suffered, yes, but for *our* sakes. God could not have forsaken man without destroying him. The Creator, the Mediator of Life, and the Agent of Life, suffered because of, and in behalf of, our rebellion against the self in God. Forgiveness from God is offered. Pride resists forgiveness. Forgiveness damns fetishes. Forgiveness apprehended and experienced provides personal liberty to adore God instead of fetishes. Forgiveness, received and appreciated, is the basis for understanding ourselves and the needs of other men. Forgiveness enables the new self to love life while seeing it realistically, to grant men freedom while being wounded by their folly.

Forgiveness enables the new man to live the life of self-esteem amid the paradoxes. The spirit of death, the spirit of evil, the devil, threatens man with an atom of truth and declares that there are no paradoxes. Thus, the need for dependence and losing one's life is poisoned into escapism and neurotic dependence. The fact of self-love is cheapened into conceit. The need for self-confidence is disguised as arrogance. The need for self-esteem is cheapened to mean rigid pride. The need for individuality is exploited to mean neurotic detachment. The need for discernment is thwarted to a form of pharisaism. The need for redemptive love is prostituted into an unrestrained sexual narcotic.

The soul experiencing self-realization, however, is able to come to terms with what seems at first inconsistent. With the self disguised, he was threatened by the command to lose an already lost self. Now he has the power to deny even legitimate desires of self in order to take up the cross of higher purpose.

Previously he was told that hostility was absolutely sinful and repulsive. Now the emerging self enables the ego to express hostility when necessary, and channel aggression into constructive uses.

Previously he was told that he suffered because he idolized persons, leaned on them too heavily, and made them responsible for his life. He was not even aware when they were stultifying him and using him to base ends. Now he can return to the forbidden land and trust persons, even giving them the right to hurt him because he loves.

Previously he was told he was making a fetish of some kind in his work. Now he can return to the job, work tirelessly, and live out the calling of Christian vocation.

Previously he made a god of his father, overlooking all faults, and seeing only a superman to bring him safety and salvation. Now he can go to his father and "touch the fire," honoring his father, seeing his many faults but not seeing them, loving him for what he is despite all that he has revealed of himself.

Previously he was told that he thought of parties, comfort, and good times entirely too much. Now he can enjoy himself without guilt, and can choose his amusements wisely without feeling he has betrayed the Man of Sorrows.

The world will understand the church's witness when it is clear what we mean. When we speak of the "salvaging of personality," we do not mean a renunciation of true being, but the recovery of it. We do not mean the suffocation of the self, but the discovery of it. We do not mean the end of the ego, but the harnassing of its powers. To surrender to the Spirit of Christ does not mean the loss of identity, but the finding of it. When the Bible says "And he died for all, that those who live might live no longer for themselves but for him who for their sake died and was raised" (II CORINTHIANS 5:15), this does not imply the end of individuality, but its beginning. (The new life is not introverted toward a bleeding self, but outward from a whole self.) And lastly, to be obedient to God does not mean running away from life, but walking back into it.

The new man may be justly proud. The self may be legitimately satisfied with persons or projects which exist in their own right and are not possessed by him for his benefit. There is a fruitful relationship between the new man and Christ, but principally because He offers forgiveness, thereby enabling the new man to stand on his own two feet a free and courageous person. Egotism—the concentration of all ego functions on the furbishing of fetishes—whistles in the dark and meets the frightening end of William Ernest Henley. Others are proud of Christ, because in bondage to the Spirit of the Lord are they led into the light of liberty.

Out of the light that dazzles me,
  Bright as the sun from pole to pole,
I thank the God I know to be
  For Christ, the Conqueror of my soul.

Since His the sway of circumstance
  I would not wince nor cry aloud—
Under that rule which men call chance
  My head with joy is humbly bowed.

Beyond this place of sin and tears
  That life with Him! and His the aid,
Despite the menace of the years,
  Keeps, and shall keep me, unafraid.

I have no fear, though strait the gate,
  He cleared from punishments the scroll;
Christ is the Master of my fate,
  Christ is the Captain of my soul.

—Dorothea Day

Over the years I have witnessed wonderful victories of human life, each person seeing at last that meekness is not timidity, and that "we are more than conquerors through Him who loved us." I have always been aghast at the number of dropouts in church, because between the ages of 14 and 19 is a critical period in understanding the importance of self-appreciation.

I remember Jerry. Jerry came from a home in which both father and mother were Christians. Father thought he was doing the boy a favor by demanding the highest grades in school and by hinting what a wonderful thing it would be if Jerry became a medical missionary. It is no surprise that Jerry's dad disliked himself for not appearing more important in life.

Jerry tried hard. But he fell into a failure pattern. He developed an ulcer, and began to have headaches. Father became unhappy. Jerry worked harder.

One evening the authorities visited the home to pick Jerry up for stealing an automobile with several others in his gang. Imagine the ranting and raving at home that evening.

Jerry came to my office regularly for conferences. There seemed to be little he could say concerning his past life. The self had been persecuted by impossible expectations, and as a consequence decided it wasn't worth the effort to be a person.

"I'm always getting into trouble," he moaned.

"Don't worry," I replied. "Some of the finest people I know have been causing trouble these days. It all depends on why you're causing it."

"I don't think my father ever expects me to amount to much. Maybe now he'll see that he can quit bugging me. I don't think I'm worth the effort."

Now that Jerry was guilty, he thought even less of himself. He claimed to receive God's forgiveness, but he was still listless. He slumped in his chair.

One morning I said, "Jerry, would you try something for me? It is simple: (*1*) every time you sit in a chair try and grow one inch; (*2*) every morning for one month stand straight as you can alone, and say Romans 8:31,32 aloud; and (*3*) every evening in your prayers pray for your parents, place yourself in God's hands, and say to the Lord, 'Lord, thank you for making me a somebody.' "

Time passed, and Jerry decided to become a truck driver. He got through school with average grades and became an active member of the union. He is a credit to the Lord. It is amazing to this day how he sits in a chair. It is as though an iron pole were strapped to his back. Someone actually remarked, "Jerry sits as if he is someone."

"Naturally!" I replied.

3

A Hale and Holy You

YOUR INDIVIDUALITY IS the one contribution you can make to the whole world, at a time when it seems least in demand. The mass market of produce and politics demand that you be predictable. Cooperation is beginning to resemble regimentation. We are worried about finding thinking space at a time when the population explosion threatens our living and eating habits. For a brief moment a philosopher expounds the glory of individualism, but most of the time such behavior appears too unprofitable, if not downright risky. The individual is interesting as a theological phenomenon, but valuable thereafter only as an economic statistic or a political pawn.

We Christians have partially helped make things worse. The glory of individuality is hailed as uniqueness, the ability to be different, the art of being odd and liking it.

As a matter of fact, who wants to be different? Take a small crowd where the people are acting and looking the same; probably only two or three are fully individuals. Which ones? Appearances will not say. The fact that God made snowflakes and tree leaves all different is not the basis of our individuality.

The nonconformist is often racing madly from the inner urge to be completely compliant. Beatniks as a group toss society into the ashcan, but among themselves their idiosyncrasies must be spun off the mimeographed "base plan for oddballs." Adolescents are "individualists" at home and dots in a rigid herd outside. No, outward differences tell us little about the extent of individuality.

Uniqueness for itself may be the prelude to egotism run wild.

The urge to think up one's own destiny and write homemade laws lead to the hope that we shall answer to no one but ourselves. The mass mind, however, prides itself on preferring safety to that madness.

If "individuality" is not necessarily being different, then what is it? It is grateful acceptance of all your God-given functions and skills. It is realization that the marvel of you was created through Christ, and that you must do the will of God by authenticating the integrity of yourself. "Individuality" is buoyant affirmation of your life and its powers. The rich range of your personality keyboard comes into its own when in harmony with "international pitch," and you are attuned to the Spirit of Christ.

The "old self" (ROMANS 6:6) is essentially a false personality, a self dominated by one or more fetishes. This self must be denied, canceled out, unmasked (MARK 8:34). The constricted man glories in these fetishes. For him they are shortcuts to universal harmony and the distinctiveness of one's own pride. The Spirit of all life seeks to reveal the futility of this fatal course, and that the persistently sinful man loses harmony both with a larger life and with his own individual self.

The neurotic personality may or may not be possessed by the Spirit of life in Christ.

The so-called more "normal" personality outside of Christ is not so rigidly bound by an image of himself as a universally perfect and omnipotent god (as is the neurotic). He is more of an actor. He gives himself to small groups (which I call "microworlds"). He finds glory in these. They accept his obedience and honor him with the security of acceptance.

One of the great threats of our modern age is that the standards of each microworld are advertised and inculcated over wide areas by mass communication. The lost man knows full well what is required of each microworld in his week's existence. Like magic appears the Independent Man, the Social Man, the Ambitious Man, the Family Man, the Religious Man, the Respectable Man, the Sexual Man, and you name it. The neurotic is plagued by blind rage that the world will not believe him. The lost soul is haunted by the despair of not believing himself.

Watson's system of psychology, called "behaviorism," never

enthused men of science for long, but he did dwell on some insights we have not fully appreciated. Any of us may learn whole sets of personalities, whole habit systems which are flashed on and off as if by a light-switch. We seek out areas of living where we are comfortable with the code. Fashion dictates truth, the production has been rehearsed often, and the mind flips up its "idiot cards" as we slip comfortably into the smooth spiel, or the sales pitch, or the hep talk, or the party line.

The constricted man looks at the institutional church and has no desire to be converted when it means slipping into one more costume, called the "Church Man." The idolatry of the church is an attempt to make it easier for him by converting the kingdom to one or more microworlds, minimizing the need for a new, radical adjustment. James' question was never more searching: "Do you not know that friendship with the world is enmity with God?" (JAMES 4:4).

We have said that the lost soul throws himself into each new venture in the hope of finding salvation. He soon becomes listless and cynical. This gives a good example of the reason why episodes of sexuality mobilize such screaming appeal. Word is whispered that sexual indulgence is the key to self-fulfillment. At the same time, many news-, book-, and drug-stores are overflowing with incredibly vile trash, endorsing certain kinds of sexual experiences as the keys to life. The microworld of perverted sexual promiscuity grows wider in appeal. This means that in addition to the innate sexual drive calling for satisfaction, The Sexual Man-About-Town now invests the security of the entire self in the code of a micro-world which promises both acceptance and glory. The game is played lustily—if you will pardon the word—because in this case the very personal nature of the experience holds out the additional hope of gaining individuality. But placing the whole ego "on the line" in the idolatry of sex results in a gambler's loss so heavy that there is no turning back. Innate drive and family instinct may eventually be so completely garbled and twisted that all is utterly a Big Production, but alienation from the microworld and from a society which idolizes the sexual role constitutes a threat so black that the game must be played to its bitter end of moral and spiritual bankruptcy.

The experience of being translated from one microworld to another is one of self-subtraction. The lost man feels splintered, shattered, divided, diminished; very little is left that represents all of him. Cynicism—the opposite of faith—is listlessness in play-acting and a smirk at those who take themselves seriously. In Ephesians it is declared that the self gets down to nothing, until it must be considered dead: "And you he made alive, when you were dead through the trespasses and sins in which you once walked, following the course of this world . . ." (EPHESIANS 2:1,2). The microworld sings "For He's a Jolly Good Fellow," and the glory-addict often feels as though he is standing somewhere off to the side while the crowd is singing to someone else. No part of him speaks for all of him.

Parts of him "do their stuff" for the crowd, but it is as if someone pressed the button, a motor turned over, and he follows the prescribed course. His pride in adulation becomes a calloused "dividuality." He finds it increasingly difficult to laugh at himself, and trivial matters are blown up to gigantic proportions. The date at the party, the new tablecloth, the color of the car, a TV program, someone's remark, or vacation preparations—these become matters of cosmic consequence. His fate rides on the consummation of the trivial.

The longing to be at home with all parts of his true being is a search for wholeness. The most universal of all temporary measures to bind the constricted man into wholeness are two-fold: be at home in the "right" microworlds, or to be above them all. The first is classless morality; the second respectability.

Conditioning of morality is big business. They tell me that in the spring of 1966, London is so far in it's almost out. The scenes of dynamic, chic, scintillating vulgarity are a succession of film clips, and you can make each scene—"There's a whole scene going"—with no trouble at all. Says *Time*: "In fact, there is not one London scene, but dozens. Each one is a dazzling gem, a medley of checkered sunglasses and delightfully quaint pay phone boxes, a blend of 'flash' American, polished Continental and robust old English influence that mixes and merges in London today." A cosmopolitan city is one in which the microworlds are not too hard on each other. Richard Adler, editor of London's *Town Magazine*, says that London is "far more accessible than anywhere else. In New

York, Paris and Rome, actors, writers and so on each have their own little groups, their little street packs. If you put your toe in the wrong square, you get stepped on. In London, everyone parties with everyone."

Recently I remarked during a lecture that the inside of the microcosm is completely lined with mirrors so that the inmates can keep check on how they're doing. I got a chuckle out of reading in the same issue of *Time*, "At these and dozens of other discothèques, beautiful gals with long blonde hair and slimly handsome men go gracefully through their explosive, hedonistic, totally individual dances, surrounded by mirrors so that they can see what a good time they're having."

Respectability is on the other end of the spectrum. It is a distant, covert "peace" with all roles, all segments of society, all microworlds. *Respectability* prides itself on wholeness in a vacuum, and seeks to avoid the demands of God on the one hand and the invitation to the despair of the microworlds on the other. When it meets Christianity, it is much like two women who meet at the ball wearing exactly the same clothes. They stare icily at each other. "Humpf!" growls the Christian; "Cheap counterfeit of reality!"

"Humpf!" retorts *respectability* huffily; "Unnatural distortion of the free spirit!"

But, as anyone who has done evangelistic visitation will tell you, The Respectable American has no argument with God, only with *excess respectability*. He worships the Ten Commandments and The Golden Rule, and is amazed himself at all the things he doesn't do. What he can't stand is excess sin or excess goodness.

In reference to the case of John Profumo and Christine Keeler of England, *Time* magazine printed the following comment: "The upright men among England's Top People live morally because a gentleman should do so, and not, so it seems, because the church tells them to. And among the passionate playboys of Mayfair—as the Profumo case suggests—a mention of the ethical teachings of the Church of England would seem an astonishing irrelevancy."

Those committed to the religion of *respectability* have lost their individuality and submerged true being, because, as in all roles played in concert, the central task is keeping native members in line. If the "home team" goes up in smoke, there is no place to go but to some stupid microworld—perish the thought! In commenting on the Profumo affair, novelist Rebecca West said, "The problem is, as it always has been, to get the goats and monkeys under control. The Ward case is a problem in animal training, and we are the animals." In other words, two men were a sorry mess because they betrayed the "club."

Both moral indifference and *respectability* demonstrate the impossibility of escaping the despair of splintered being. Life's lessons of no refuge and no joy are lost on the unredeemed person who still anticipates the messianic state. The rise of Naziism in Germany was an event flowering from seed planted by generations of philosophers, poets, and theologians who saw in the people's pride in the fatherland the one overarching loyalty capable of binding together the fragments of broken personality.

Persons of keen sensitivities and skills have envisioned the altruistic cause as the eternal cohesive to bind the human spirit into one. How can we bind so many of diverse skills and temperaments into one spirit of understanding and brotherhood? Too frequently those with "the dream" are unable to teach us. Albert Einstein had two rules for living: (*1*) have no rules, and (*2*) always think independently. He often remarked that he didn't want anything from anyone. Einstein, a universal spirit, could not bring persons to both their own individuality and the universal spirit through his own personal pattern of life.

Erich Fromm has correctly analyzed, with deep feelings, the dilemma of modern man attempting to find universal identity on the one hand, and his own individuality on the other. He says, "The 'organization man' may be well fed, well amused and well oiled, yet he lacks a sense of identity because none of his feelings or his thoughts originates within himself; none is authentic. He has no convictions, either in politics, religion, philosophy or in love. He is attracted by the 'latest model' in thought, art and style, and lives under the illusion that the thoughts and feelings which he has acquired by listening to the media of mass communication are his own.

"He has a nostalgic longing for a life of individualism, initiative and justice, a longing that he satisfies by looking at Westerns. But these values have disappeared from real life in the world of giant corporations, giant state and military bureaucracies and giant labor unions. He, the individual, feels so small before these giants that he sees only one way to escape the sense of utter insignificance: He identifies himself with the giants and idolizes them as the true representatives of his own human powers, those of which he has dispossessed himself."

When he addresses himself to the solution, Fromm begins with a remarkably faithful feeling for the nature of man. He demonstrates that self-interest is fundamental to self-realization, and that self-love is not selfishness. He says, "It follows that man can deceive himself about his real self-interest if he is ignorant of his self and its real needs. . . ." So far, so good. His aim is for the man who "loves life, who has faith in life, who is productive and independent."

Where then does Fromm take us? Down the garden path to the charm of rainbows and the perfume of rare roses! He is so adept at misunderstanding John Calvin and making wild accusations that religion causes suffocation of the self, that his solution must look to a humanist industrialism, a social rearrangement! Let us finish the above partial quote: "It follows that man can deceive himself about his real self-interest if he is ignorant of his self and its real needs and that the science of man is the basis for determining what constitutes man's self-interest."

The "science of man"? What is *that*? We do not know what it is, or how it proposes to help each individual find the faith and power to affirm the broad scope of his potential. The science of man? What science? What man? By its very nature, such a thing is impossible, but Fromm refers to it as an actuality, and says it should be used to transform our social system from a managed industrialism into an industrialism favoring man's potentialities, "those of love and of reason." That is the trouble with the whole history of mankind. No doubt there is something wrong, and no doubt a solution would be better than the dilemma, but how is anyone's social rearrangement going to fit the needs of all individuals, and who is to do the rearranging? And how will the arrangement fit the needs of changing ages? And how will the arrangement inform the individual where he can find faith for his love and hope for his work? How will any arrangement enable each self to accept and forgive the selves which differ so radically from his own? What science will provide a cleansing justification from the very Source of creation for the failure to realize the goals of universal love and self-actualization when once we have the courage to envision these goals? And what science will provide man with the hope for universal love and unity when Marxist-culture quackery and all other contrived panaceas fail the tests of history?

Why Fromm insists that the failures of the institutional church are the last word about the validity of the Christian faith we do not know. We do know, however, that the fact of the spirit of life in Christ is history's tested avenue to both the actualization of the individual and the society of individuals in grateful concert. We have faith in man because of the nature of his creation, and because a means is provided for man to have faith in himself and his fellows. The agency of creation, justification, and universal hope for the future is found in one Being in Christian faith: the Spirit of life.

The salvation of all societies cannot exist apart from the salvation of individuals, and universal salvation is not an event we look for so long as history takes into account the present mixture of the individual's sin and freedom.

What the Christian faith does affirm is that both the world and the redeemed and redeeming culture can exist together. By not superimposing its arrangement on the world, the church esteems more faith in the individual than he is aware of. The church is not selling a system. It calls for the realization of the self through Christ, and then has faith in the power of the individual to prize the system which is most in accord with his new faith and freedom.

Robert Louis Stevenson once said, "To be what we are, and to become what we are capable of becoming, is the only end of life." The Westminster Catechism states: "The chief end of man is to glorify God and enjoy Him forever." These two statements are complementary. This was demonstrated in the incarnation, identification, death, resurrection, and ascension of Jesus Christ. This is personally validated in the individual's embrace of the Spirit of life in Christ. It is this Spirit of holiness which brings the individual to his Creator for spiritual rebirth and a sharing of the divine nature. Science gives light. And in Christ's life is the world's light.

Looking past the noise and annoyances, one can observe growing children struggle to be themselves in the competing worlds of the routine day. In our home we try to air feelings and think through the Bible in terms of our experiences. A recent session was unusually significant. We were seated around the table, meditating on the phrase in Acts 10:38: ". . . he went about doing good . . . for God was with him."

One of us wondered how Jesus could continually do good since He, too, knew such emotions as fear, disappointment, and pain, as well as such feelings as hunger, thirst, fatigue, and sorrow. Another wondered if perhaps Jesus just kept thinking about His duty. I asked what the family thought was the basis of continually doing good. The eleven-year-old responded, "I'm sure it was Jesus' love. He had a lot of love for most everyone. He loved them, and God, too."

I then asked how he was getting on with his own loving. He replied that tight little cliques of school chums edged him out of certain activities. Sometimes they took advantage of him when he offered friendship or invited them to something special. Then we discussed the peril of hoping that some group will take care of us and do our thinking if we give it unthinking obedience.

The boy felt deeply about all this. We talked about it. The younger fellow pounced on the discussion with the sudden realization that he himself was suspicious of boys who wanted to be eternal buddies in a few minutes. He said he tried to do his best, but had no grudge against the boys who didn't particularly like him. Mother commented that a boy ought to respect himself, and you can't force someone to like you if he doesn't want to. Someone observed that the verse said, ". . . for God was with him," and Jesus could always tell God about it when someone disappointed Him. I observed that the verse also says, "how God anointed Jesus of Nazareth with the Holy Spirit and with power. . . ." No doubt God can give us a supply of love even when people don't return love or when we don't feel like we want to love them. We prayed. No great problems were solved, but we were together in thinking about our condition as a family which wants to love like Jesus loves. Together we shared the one life; and yet each would have to live his own life as he saw fit.

Christ recovered holiness for men when their wholeness was shattered. He gave the world back to men by revealing the transcendence of the one God, at the time when they had made a god of this world. And at a time when men thought life was no greater than their fetishes, Christ revealed the glory of God through the fullness of life.

The distinct contributions of the Old Testament are in the revelation of the transcendent nature of the sovereign God and the responsibility of man as His creation, summarized in the doctrine of holiness. Holiness, for God, is the self-affirmation of all His attributes, expressed in the unity of His transcendent and infinite Being. His is the one rule which shatters all divisive thrones. It is the one glory which makes a shambles of every competing microworld. It is the one demonstration of power which stultifies every pompous display.

In the Person of Christ, holiness is pure humanity, which illumines every concealment of the human spirit from its eternal life. In the redemption of Christ, holiness is given to those who recognize their divided allegiances. Holiness, for persons, is the sharing of the divine nature, a growing freedom in the Spirit of life, and an unfolding awareness of wholeness in mind and body. A holy individual is one who is grateful for the power to be hale and hearty.

As a delicate organ of life with an infinite number of spiritual facets (most unknown even to himself), man has been almost destroyed by sin. He is not holy in and of himself. Holiness is from God. "You shall be holy, for I am holy" (I PETER, I:16). He complains that he lost his individuality because the roles he played in his microworlds were thrust on him by circumstances. He may argue that respectability is a cultural salvation, all right, but he had to work sedulously to claim it. He may argue that pain and suffering never spoke to him the inherent sermons some claim to hear, and the vicarious release of his hostility and frustration against life is through such innocent satisfactions as TV and the theater. He may argue that the institutional church disguised God, "the celestial blob," as God, the Business Executive, in a gray flannel robe. He may even argue with pride that he prizes the only individuality made possible to him—a family, guarded by faithfulness and nourished with self-sacrificing love.

Very well. The Christian man does not claim that the joy and victory of the life in Christ are experienced in direct proportion to the prior depths of self-hate and defeat, else we incorrectly accuse human love and respectability of being the enemies of the Gospel. We readily admit that lost men cannot be persuaded to appreciate that which they have never tasted. And we readily admit that the holiness of the one God appears utterly irrelevant to the succession of plotless dramas called the "daily routine."

We do say, however, that the atonement of Jesus did not take place on Venus or Mars. He lived in the marketplaces of crowded cities and knew who He was right up to His death and resurrection. In His temptations He had to decide whether He would be the Holy One of Israel, according to God's holiness, or act the role of a mob messiah, according to the wishful thinking of the people. "For we have not a high priest who is unable to sympathize with our weaknesses, but one who in every respect has been tempted as we are, yet without sinning" (HEBREWS 4:15). He died because He was in possession of Himself. Knowing no other Self than the one in God, He had no other refuge than God; therefore, when role-players killed Him, God raised Him from the dead and bestowed on Him the name which is above every name. Because of this resurrection, we say that the true life in God is "eternal," and that eternity is illumined by radiant hope only for those who are in love with life.

We will go even further and admit that when lost men catch a glimpse of the fullness of individual selfhood in Christ, they do not of themselves have the power to reach out for wholeness. No, we must insist, as the Bible proclaims, that life is not something grabbed, but created, and not devised, but born into. Therefore, it must be God in us, the Holy Spirit, who unfetters us from the shackles of pride, while all those on the stage with us, and all those in the audience, glare in astonishment at our betrayal of the drama in which we once yearned to be a star.

"Hypocrite!"

The taunts are there, spoken or not. Those around us know us by the reactions we stimulate in them. They are uncomfortable when we step out of our world and theirs. "What's with you, friend? Are you getting a touch of religion or something?"

The final cry: "We know you!"

This is the piercing taunt. Not because it is true, but because it isn't. God knows who we are. These friends accommodated themselves to the persons we gave them. God would not be so easily satisfied. He who insists on Himself will insist on ourselves. The world will be shocked that this insistence means betrayal of its false gods, and will then be embarrassed when we turn about to serve the world. This time we insist on following the living God, not in order for men to tell us who we are (the Spirit of life is revealing that), but, rather, that we might enable men to discover who they are. God gives us this freedom, that we might give this freedom to neighbors. Courage to be ourselves means increasing freedom for those we live with, whether or not they immediately appreciate our integrity or their enlarged liberty.

I have known many people, but a few stand out in my memory. One was my piano teacher. She "feasted" on every day, down to the last morsel. She lived wholeheartedly.

People noticed her because her clothes were old—not a year or two old, but really old, though always perfectly clean. They were good clothes. She never had time to buy new ones. Or maybe she didn't have the money. She spent quite a bit of money traveling to the homes of her pupils, sometimes in a bus, or in a trolley or a cab. She was usually late. She never knew when to leave. Lessons were an hour long, which meant that we had an hour at the piano; then we spent almost another hour talking about life and its meaning.

On a typically snowy, stormy day, she would rush in like a whirlwind. "Isn't it a perfectly magical day! Have you ever seen it so gloriously white and invigorating and thrilling?"

I would look at the dirty sludge and reply, "Yes. Thrilling." It was a strange sight to see her fingers racing over the keyboard, her big hat flopping, and her long dress, which was down to her ankles.

Those were good clothes. She was married to the publisher of a New York newspaper. He died and left her a spacious home in Brooklyn. She wanted to prove something to herself, so she went into "the game," as she called it, meaning "the newspaper game." She was editor of the society page; and she traveled around in high-class society.

She was a believer—not a superficial believer, but a deep believer. She believed what God told her, and she staked her whole life on it. She had the feeling that Jesus Christ wanted her to do something different for a vocation. Out of a clear blue sky she understood what He was saying, and, since that was the order for the day, she simply did it. The house was sold, she took a small upstairs flat in that area of south Brooklyn where "a tree grew," and she went about teaching piano.

I kept taking lessons, even though as a pianist I was a better juggler. I stayed on because she often said that I was "absolutely tremendous," and I believed it, against my better judgment. I kept on because I needed her energy. Late at night she would rush in, see my yawn, and give me a lecture: "You think you're tired. It is all in your mind. You're alive; God's life is flowing through you; you are filled to overflowing with life and power. It is wonderful, isn't it?"

I wanted to say, "You are making it up, and no, I'm bushed, and you are, too," but I didn't. She was between 80 and 85 years of age, and I knew that she had to be getting her energy from somewhere. It didn't look very good for a healthy young man to be barely hanging on, while she outdid Horowitz, so I became animated, too, and we both made plenty of noise.

"You know," she would look up and say, "last night I lost my needle. I said, 'Well now, what good does it do for me to lose a needle at this time of night, Lord? Now, you know where it is, and if you tell me where it is we'll both know, then I won't hurt myself, and I'll be able to save time since it's getting late anyway.' "

"And did He tell you where it was?" I asked.

"What do you think?"

"Well, He seems to tell you everything, so I guess He did."

"You are right. I promptly forgot all about it, and a little later this voice said to me, 'Why don't you look behind the sofa?' And I wanted to say, 'Why, what would it be doing back there, Lord?' But naturally I looked, and. . . ."

"There it was," I said.

"Right again. Well, I certainly thanked Him, and it is peace of mind knowing you're never alone."

It is strange how distinctly I remember her words to me.

Sometimes right in the middle of a piece she would make a comment. When I have had trouble, I could almost hear her saying, "Don't worry. Think clearly, pray, do the very best you can, and let God handle the rest. God wants people to do the very best they can and then sleep well at night." And then there was her strange hat. It never occurred to anyone to laugh at this old woman, who wore old clothes and lived in two small rooms, with a piano big enough for a concert hall. They laughed instead at her witty remarks. One day she was walking down the street, and God reached down and took her. Many people wept, and their hearts have still not healed.

She was surely an individual, if there ever was one.

4

The Man with the Way to Life

THE CENTRAL TASK of Christianity is to make good the promise, "And this is what he has promised us, eternal life" (I JOHN 2:25).

The world's libraries of philosophy and religion offer a better life. Many insights about man and the nature of things are offered. Why and how is Christ so unique? Why is it that the fullness of God's life comes solely through Him?

Man has such basic, inherent relations with cosmic power that we are mystified by the vastness of the larger life he reflects. We have hints that he was created with powers of transmission and reception that have fallen into disuse. It is when you realize what men could be that you recognize that most of them are more dead than alive.

For example, the mood of man is radically affected by negative and positive ions. He responds to certain ranges of light frequencies so radically that, not only his moods, but his susceptibility to disease and even to cancer may be affected. Subtle electronic frequencies given off from certain muscles are probably an unexplored means of communication, a phenomenon undoubtedly employed by the ancient mystics. As soon as we surmount the prejudice of some psychologists, we shall get to wider experimentation with the staggering possibilities of extrasensory perception.

Russia has taken the lead in experimenting with DOP (dermo-optical perception), whereby subjects perceive colors, and in some cases even read, through the fingers and other parts of the body. The Russians claim that while some persons have gifts along this line, the ability can be learned.

Today the vast powers of the unconscious mind for health and wholeness are opening up through the research of many scientists and psychiatrists, building on the work of such people as Sigmund Freud, Karen Horney, Harry Stack Sullivan, Carl Jung, and Carl Rogers.

At some time most of us have experienced a rushing up of love, power, and energy from the depths of being, to take us breathlessly out of this restriction of our mass-time-space condition. The Apostle Paul referred to such an experience, and said that it was so sublime he could not reveal the details.

The ancient mystics of other religions unlocked many of these secrets. They knew the obstructing power of hostility, conflict, and fetishness to block the interaction of human spirit with the infinite Life. They discovered that by intensive concentration upon love, unity, and the eternal Spirit, one could canalize through his spirit powers of healing, foreseeing, and persuasiveness; their actions were thought to be miraculous. These mystics were so preoccupied with the powers of spirit, that they disdained the flesh and material possessions, and were considered to be inspired by their followers.

The end result is that man is delighted with his prospects of not only controlling energy, but becoming something of a supernatural being.

The questions with which we began persist—Can one discover meaning in the cosmos solely through Christ? Can he personally experience this meaning for himself only through loyalty to Christ? Why is Christ the Lord the only Way, instead of Christ being but one of many ways? Who is to stop us from taking an unaided journey right into the heart of the universe?

The founders of man's religions did not identify themselves as the only divine vehicle. Christ did this, but for the other founders of religion the problems were accommodation to universal pain and tragedy, moral betterment, and harnassing the vast powers of the universe. But their approach was not too different from the present-day attempt to make a fetish of God by using cosmic powers in ego functioning for the benefit of an introverted and inward-looking self. To this day, the nature of the human beast is concerned with the right buttons to push to turn on the "big lights"! Have you been noticing the current slogans and sermon topics? *Prayer Gets Big Results.* Some examples are "How to Get Folks to Like You a Lot" and "Does Religion Work? You Bet!" Here's one I made up: "Achieve Peace, Be Successful, and the Sky's the Limit!" Why fail, when you can hit the jackpot? Friend, when you're talking about *God*, why settle for peanuts?

Connection with these powers at least gives us a feeling of relief that the universe is kind, if not a profound gratitude that "God is love."

The basic ingredients of happiness are available to all, and in matters of religion it seems that one concoction may be tastier than another. After one wipes his mouth of the morsels, the question is, "Now what interesting thing shall we do?"

The life, satisfied at mealtimes, detects other hungers it may not know how to satisfy. Put together as a whole, man is more than an organism which prays to eat. He must reckon with the totality of the powers beyond. The most satisfying experiences of friendship, music, food, and sex leave us with haunting intimations of all that is yet beyond us. The persistent surmise of what we are missing torments us in the best and the worst of experiences.

The quest for the unity of life beckons us to the heart of the cosmos, the one Spirit of all that lives, which is somehow kin to ours. Few persons could say what they were looking for until the eternal Spirit of life clarified the questions of living *after* He gave Himself and began answering them. No one knows precisely what he is looking for until the life of the eternal Spirit finds him.

You and I are called to a life vaster than we have ever conceived. It is not until you see a mechanical box with pictures that you realize that the powers of television have been in the universe from earth's dawn. What else is here we do not know about? One is right to quest for this unity of the Spirit's life instead of grasping for a little god, who is the sum of the powers his natural self can apprehend. This unity of the one transcendent Life is Sovereign over all the facets of His universe, including the miraculous functions of man and his five, six, or perhaps ten senses.

The eternal Spirit, by accommodating Himself to the human spirit, provides life's blessing and yet more than all of the single satisfactions of human existence. Natural man, at his purest, longs for love *plus* the Source of all love; reaches out to other men *and* to the Spirit for all men; hungers for reality *plus* the Wisdom of all worlds; wants goodness *and* the supreme Joy of Perfection; desires accomplishment *and* the experience of full consummation; thirsts for reconciliations *and* the summation of all things in the fullness and unity of the Creator. The pinnacle of the subjective deductions of other religions is in the realization that the Source of truth and perfect love is in the one transcendent God.

It is not written in the New Testament that Jesus came to tell us more about this God, but that as God's Son He came to bring abundant life. Life comes through His person and atonement, as well as His words. He is of our flesh and blood. It was near a crowd He was born, in crowds He taught, in the marketplace He lived, among men of all classes and conditions He ate and drank and rested, to all in need He freely bent His soul, and in the midst of a roaring mob and between two thieves He was crucified. His own life was the divine interaction of time and eternity; He immersed Himself fully in the rising and ebbing of His own and all men's lifetimes, and in return received upon His own heart the mighty outpouring of our hopes and dreams, pain and tears. They called Him the "Son of Man," and saw in Him the Soul of their own souls at their purest. Men loved Him because they are born to love life; in Him was life.

He is called the "*Alpha*" and "*Omega*," the "Creation" and the "Fulfillment," the "Beginning" and the "Completion." He covers the spectrum of our struggles. Those questing for the *Alpha*, the incarnation of the Spirit of God, find their homage in the *Omega*, the Holy Spirit of Christ in union with our spirits. The witnesses of earth, beginning with those of the Bible, did not say that they would be increasingly salvaged by the infusion of His divine powers; they said that they were already saved, because all of this eternal Spirit could dwell in any human spirit the moment the personality's avenue was opened. And the fact of continuing and final salvation did not detract from the security of full sonship from the beginning of this union.

It would do us very little good if, for some reason beyond us, the man Jesus opened more of Himself to this Spirit. If Jesus has been the center of the church's affections and dedication for these many years, it is because Jesus is *this very Spirit*, meeting us in terms we can understand and offering us this eternal life by sacrifices that would remove the defeating obstacles. It was not enough for Jesus to say that He manifested God. He added, "For as the Father raises the dead and gives them life, so also the Son gives life to whom he will" (JOHN 5:21). The man who was quite religious, but was radically changed when he encountered the Spirit of life, said, "If the Spirit of him who raised Jesus from the dead dwells in you, he who raised Christ Jesus from the dead will give life to your mortal bodies also through his Spirit which dwells in you" (ROMANS 8:11). Paul knows this Spirit; He is the "Spirit of Christ" (ROMANS 8:9).

A brilliant scientist had been conversing with me regularly. He complained that the zest was draining out of him. He could hardly force himself to do even the most necessary duties. Former pleasures were now such a chore; he was losing friends and forfeiting opportunities for betterment. The sky was permanently overcast.

His pride was self-righteousness. The truth came first—at least, he thought it did. He was a little perturbed that even when he caught insights about himself, he was unable to do much about it.

At one session we talked about his safety devices. His strictures were self-protective measures. Confidence was based on his ability to wall himself off against enemies . . . and, unfortunately, to fortify himself against love. No one could hurt or betray him. So he hoped.

Not knowing how to love persons, he flattered, cajoled, ignored, used, cornered, leaned heavily upon, or threatened them. Their spirits eluded his, and he wandered in desert places.

Then I asked him what he thought about Christ being crucified for love's sake. We discussed Christ's decision (revealed in His baptism) to be identified with all the people, and how, in sharing their lives, He was crucified by their sins. Theirs and ours. Then we dwelt on the power of God to raise those who suffer in genuine love. God raised Jesus. "If you will pardon the language," I said, "God with Christ took a terrible beating, but (referring to the resurrection) the Bible says He was 'vindicated in the Spirit.' " (I TIMOTHY 3:16).

This educated man then made an amazing statement. He said, "I suppose I never understood Christianity. I always began by arguing about some point of the creed. I can see that this Jesus is the man with the way to live."

"Quite true," I answered. "But He is still doing little for you. Your spirit is still divorced from His Spirit. Your weak love is separated from the love of God's Spirit. Christ has yet to become for you the Man with the way to life." We sat in silence while he considered his responsibility for the next decision.

It is because we receive life from Him that He is designated as "*the* Source," and not merely an Example. He is not a Means to resurrection; He is called "*the* Resurrection." His is not just one of many ways to live; He is "the Life." He is not just a good Person; He is our "Righteousness." He is not just a Means to wholeness; He is our "Sanctification."

In Christ's day, men wished to use Him as a magical Avenue to awesome power for themselves and their nation. His central problem was to turn their eyes away from the utopian Messiah to the Messiah, Servant of the people. Men could always get more out of life, with or without a bit more religion. But to lay hold on *the eternal life* would usher in the satisfaction of forever living in the total life, total purpose, and total power of God, for one moment and forever. If hunger for life brings us to the glory of God, we can have all the life we were created for, but if the protection of lesser life is our glory, then we lose both life and the glory for which it was made.

We are forever indebted to the Jewish people for imparting the revelation that man exists for the glory of God, and not vice versa. The entire purpose of this covenant people was to identify God. He was named, identified, described, studied, talked to, obeyed, followed. The more men knew about the purposes of God, the more they learned about themselves.

"Woe is me! For I am lost; for I am a man of unclean lips . . . for my eyes have seen the King, the Lord of hosts!" (ISAIAH 6:5).

The symbol for all that identified the eternal God was His name. Specifically, it conveyed a mighty, immediate Presence, the here-and-now power and holiness of God Himself. Jesus was the final and clearest Expression of that name. To see Jesus is to see the "Father of spirits" (HEBREWS 12:9; see also NUMBERS 16:22). The matters of the New Testament were written ". . . that you may believe that Jesus is the Christ, the Son of God, and that believing you may have life in his name" (JOHN 20:31).

The nature of man now partakes of the nature of the Spirit of life in Christ, and the new man, at home with all men, is most at home with his unique self.

"His divine power has granted to us all things that pertain to life and godliness, through the knowledge of him who called us to his own glory and excellence, by which he has granted to us his precious and very great promises, that through these you may escape from the corruption that is in the world because of passion, and become partakers of the divine nature" (II PETER 1:3,4).

In Acts 2 and elsewhere, the divine power of God for human life is clearly identified as the "holy Spirit of Christ." Here is the crux of the matter. How can men know that the infinite Power hovering over their soul is the Spirit of life in Christ? It is the Spirit Himself who must first touch men with the recognition that His eternal nature is revealed as the nature, the personality, of Jesus Christ. The Bible clearly states that one cannot declare Jesus to be universal Lord except by the power of the Spirit (see I CORINTHIANS 12:3).

The resurrection makes the clearly identified Spirit of life in Christ available to sinful human spirits. The New Testament declares that the salvation of man is enabled by both the death and the resurrection of Jesus, and that is why the slogan we see on signs and car bumpers, "Christ died for our sins," is an oversimplification. It stimulates the oft-heard question, "What has that got to do with me now?" The writers of the New Testament did not say that man's relationship with the eternal Spirit was made possible solely through Christ's death.

Dr. Floyd V. Filson writes: "This may seem to point to the

Cross as the central fact upon which to base our presentation of the biblical message. Yet the conclusion is completely false. None of the New Testament books, none of the New Testament sermons, none of New Testament thinking was centered in the Cross. . . . That central fact should now be clear. The interpreting clue and the organizing fact of biblical theology is the resurrection of Jesus."

What we are saying, then, is that our basic concern is not with ourselves, but with Christ *living*. We are drawn not to nameless powers of the universe, but to Christ, the Power of God. He is our *Life*. By yielding every act and thought to the Spirit of life in Christ, we find a deep kinship with all those who are alive to their fingertips, and we are found resisting all that suffocates the yearning of each spirit to live.

When the distortions of sin are erased, we treasure the unity that makes for the bond of peace, and we respect the gifts which reveal the unique powers of the individual. Christ is Lord of all men, just as the Spirit of life in Christ is the reigning and transcendent Spirit, whether or not men have opened themselves to Him. The powers we derive from the Spirit of Christ could not be used contrary to either the nature of man or the nature of God.

God's might must come through the Lord Jesus Christ. Our uniqueness must be implemented through the Christ of all men. The New Testament enjoins us to pray in the name of Christ, sifting requests through His personality, expecting answers by His power, impelled toward goals ordained by His will.

Selfish concentration on the gifts of divine power makes for that faceless conformity which so characterizes the Eastern religions. But a meeting of hearts in Christ makes for a rich diversity, which demonstrates to us clearly that the God and Father of Jesus Christ is a sovereign and personal Being who, as infinite Spirit, can give an infinite amount of Himself to an infinite number of people.

Religion has historically employed faceless conformity as the means for depersonalizing the painful aspects of living. To thwart and sublimate the tumultuous passions, religionists have employed the straitjackets of familiar religious phrases, universal garb for men and women, prescribed methods of acting "religiously," and religious "hideouts" where we can escape the evil and misery around us.

This historic debasement of human nature by religion has been responsible for the problem which has vexed us because it is essentially an artificial one—namely, how can men who serve the one God be thoroughly unique in their personalities and dedicated to the trusting of both Christ and themselves. Over against this fact is the life of Jesus, who lived the life of the Holy Spirit, with all the emotions of man in all man's situations, yet without sin. He teaches us, and His Spirit gives us power, to live God's life where we are and in what we are doing.

Sending young persons into "full-time Christian service" may give them a false sense of superiority and isolation, but it gives the rest of us a bad inferiority complex, for it makes us wonder how we can glorify God and still do all the allegedly "irreligious" tasks which monopolize our time, such as making love, making "good," making friends, and making money. We see clearly that all things were created by the Spirit of life in Christ, and that all things will never be in full harmony until they are brought into concord with the mind of Christ. We need grace, the uplifting resource, God's sufficiency, and *infinite* grace, because we see in Christ's flesh and blood what we can be in the perfection of full maturity, but can never achieve in our own unaided flesh and blood.

The truth is, that peace with God and the peace of God are gifts of God's Spirit, made possible through God's "Bridge," Christ Jesus. The new man in Christ is immersed in new troubles and conflicts, but these do not result from a divided and fetish-worshipping self, and are not conflicts of continuous outright aggression, suspicion, and guilt. These are conflicts with the spirit of evil and death, which hovers so persistently over us all from the day we are born, and over which we previously had so little control; and if ours are weapons of the Spirit, out of such conflicts can arise a new fullness of God's peace.

No doubt this sense of peace often escapes us. How easy it is to feel that if the truth of life is safeguarded in a creed, all must be well with us, and the capricious souls of men are not too great a threat to the stability of our religious ways. The creeds, it is true, are vital to a common understanding of the methods of God with man. But the creeds were written by inspired men, and can only inspire other men so dedicated to the underlying truth. An unbeliever will not participate in the divine Nature by nodding to another's description of it. It cannot be implied that Christ must be known through our inspired phrases or not at all; for then the "resurrection" would be the creedal password to recognize "club members," instead of the past and present fact of God's Spirit raising human life to the life of God.

If the channel of Life is to be solely the creeds, then Christ cannot be trusted with His own Spirit to go where He will, speak to whom He will, and employ language and participate in events of His own choosing. He is found, then, to be the "Gatekeeper" of the church, and not her Lord. The creeds nowhere even intimate that this is so.

The Spirit of life in Christ employs the Bible to stimulate the yearning of men for His eternal life and to point to Christ as *the* Way and *the* Life. The Bible calls itself a "sword." The power of the Bible to bring men to life has led anxious persons to feel that the eternal Spirit is somehow encased in the book itself, and that if you safeguard the authenticity and integrity of the printed page, you place your life in a vault, where it cannot be disturbed.

Can anyone unconsciously make a fetish of the Bible? Isn't it strange that even the devil continues to quote us the Scriptures? If ancient Israel attempted to make a fetish of Jehovah in behalf of their racial pride, if the Pharisees attempted to use a good code as a fetish, if the nation of Jesus attempted to use Him as a fetish, it should not surprise us that some modern Christians audaciously claim Scripture's magical powers as their exclusive possession, because they loudly profess to be the sole group that believes every word.

The Bible does not need our defense. It is not an apologetic for the Christian faith about God and man. The Bible is the inspired and uniquely created vehicle of God, given to speak to the true manhood of our being, and to reveal the Spirit of life as the Spirit of Christ. We know the Bible is true primarily because the nature of man is able to validate what is said of the nature of God. The written Word is not a matter of public debate, because the question of whether the life, death, and resurrection of Jesus are the fullest expressions of the atoning power of love in life and of the eternal power of the Spirit over death, can be validated by the witness of the Spirit Himself in human experience. There were five hundred witnesses in the early days who could testify, under oath, that they saw the risen Christ. No one, however, succeeded pressuring Paul into accepting the fact of Christ's resurrection. But his experience of the Holy Spirit was all the proof he ever needed, and whenever he was called upon to give evidence of his faith, he usually told the story of how Christ apprehended him.

The only way men are convinced of the reality of life through the Spirit in Christ is by their personal satisfaction with what they were created for—eternal life. Our apologetic is essentially a matter of living Christ to the full, for against the joy of life there is no satisfying argument. When the Spirit of God is moving on the hearts of men and is given His freedom through the will of both God and His children, then the arguments for Christianity may be lost by debating points, and won on the streets where men are living, struggling for life, and dying for lack of it. And make no mistake, the issue is the living and dying of men. It is not because of their rationalizations concerning the trustworthiness of the Bible or the lack of it that men live or die. If they die, it is because they prefer the glory of their fetishes to the glory of God's Spirit.

If we trust deeply in Christ, it is not because we are convinced of His uniqueness by a profound book on apologetics. All of life at the deepest level of reality magnetizes us toward His personality. All universal religions describe the desirable qualities of this reality; all call on the powers of the cosmos to augment our own power to live effectively.

Only of Christ can it be claimed that the universe contains the stamp of Christ's Person on every atom. Only of Christ can it be said that in this life He touched the whole spectrum of human emotion and lived out the one Spirit of life in the flesh and blood of our so human situation. Only of Christ can it be claimed that the unity of the one Spirit of love, truth, joy, hope, and self-fullment, identified in the Messiah's flesh and blood. Only of Christ can it be demonstrated that in His resurrection He made the very Spirit of life in God available to those persons fleeing fetishes and hungering for righteousness and truth. And only of Christ can it be shown conclusively that when His life, death, and resurrection are taught, the spirit within man restlessly reaches out for the unity of life in its full-orbed purposes.

If Christ in His person and mission cannot be universally validated to the satisfaction of every man by the arbitrary pressing of high-voltage intellectual buttons, it is because the Spirit of Christ calls us to satisfactions we reject and away from sins we can cling to. Why so many are able to resist the Spirit for which their own spirits were created is a mystery. Instead of entertaining nagging doubts about the universality of the appeal of Christ's life to the spirit of all men, the apostles and church fathers before us could only assert that the sovereign God of love interacted with the limited freedom of sinful men in ways unknowable to us here and now.

It can never be said—whatever the debate over this or that miracle or circumstance in the life of Jesus—that the yearning of man's spirit created Christ out of thin air. The Lord Jesus Christ came in the flesh. He is God's gift to life. And when the Spirit of life convicts men of sin and leads them to redemption, it is to Christ they are led, and it is Christ they embrace as their example and living Lord.

When we view what God has done for our humanity, we worship the Lord who humiliated Himself for our sakes. In showing us His glory, we shall glorify Him. In giving us Christ, we shall live Christ. In conquering through grace, we shall triumph by love. All eyes and ears, all hearts and minds to Christ as we know God, to the Spirit as we experience God. The invitation of the Creator is that now we shall reverence Him, and that now and forever this gracious Lord shall be our All in All.

5

The Barker Meets Christ

THE LOSS OF God may not mean much to modern man. "God is dead! Long live mankind!" It is said that if we lose God the myth, we shall in this lonely universe have to hold on to brother man that much more tightly.

There may not be much to say in behalf of God that the humanist has not already heard, but one point ought to be made persistently—the loss of God means the loss of man.

Certainly in the rat race and the road race, in supermarkets and on superhighways, people appear to know where they're going; and it seems that what everyone needs is not more religion, but more time. People don't tell me that they have anything against God. They don't worship because they have more important things to do.

Let's study my neighbor and guess who he is. I would say he is a barker at a sideshow—he is wearing a gaudy suit, a flashy tie, and shiny shoes, he has a big hat and puffs a colossal cigar held at a rakish angle, his finger jabs the air to punctuate hair-raising comments. "Come in and see the most important, most interesting, most beautiful, most delightful, most mysterious, most. . . ."

A little crowd gathers; the people buy tickets and enter behind the curtain. They stare at a fetish. It is a crude, coarsely whittled figure of wood, which, according to the barker, has eternal and mysterious value. "There it is, folks!"

As the crowd leaves, the barker cannot look at them for embarrassment. All sideshows may be letdowns, "but the nerve!" The figure was an exact duplicate, in wood and on a small scale, of the barker himself. What a joke!

"To bad," thinks the barker. "Too bad they went in and saw. Now if there were some way to capture their interest, take their money, then distract them so that they wouldn't get behind the curtain. . . ."

Let us approach the barker and ask him who he is. His answer is that he is "that little thing in there." This is what others accept and acclaim. It is the "self" of his personality.

And so we ask him, "You mean you make a fetish of your self? Don't you ever realize it's a . . . well, a nothing?"

"It is easy for you to say that," he answers. "I worked hard to make it what it is."

"But don't you ever get suspicious? I mean, don't you ever feel that some people don't believe you, and think it's nothing but a piece of wood? Maybe somebody—maybe somebody like the girl in the fable—will say, 'Look! That's just a piece of wood!' What do you do then?"

The barker is not too happy, considering his inferiority feelings anyway, to have people call his "self" an "old piece of wood." He must admit in more lucid moments, however, that you can fool all the people some of the time—but all the people all of the time?—that *does* get to be a problem. He never is quite able to get away from the question, "Mister, if that thing in there is yourself, who are *you*?"

After awhile the barker decides, quite dramatically and with the joy of self-surrender, that he no longer is going to be a piece of wood. It was Kaijetan von Schlaggenberg who said that "Maturity consists of no longer being taken in by oneself."

It is however, so easy to believe our troubles are over if our particular fetish is what everyone needs. The two great universal "idols" of our day are sex (EPHESIANS 5:5; COLOSSIANS 3:5) and money (I TIMOTHY 6:9,10). (The Greek word translated as "covetous" actually means "adulterous" or "lascivious.") If a girl is born to be beautiful she "has it made." Just realize how many males there are who are presold on the idea that a woman should have a cute face with matching figure, and how many are in the business of enhancing both where nature has been remiss. Joe and Mabel approach each other in the fertility of their own imagination. What Mabel actually lacks physically will be more than compensated for by industry's ability to fill out reality, and by Joe's need to adore his own sexual competence. The narcotic sexual emotions, which can adjust to almost any imagined need, provide just the ring of truth about the affair. Both "barkers" are spared the *conscious* fear that when they go behind the curtain the show will be a disappointment and the facts will out. After all, love is blind.

Mabel fears self-discovery as long as she knows herself solely as a cute face with matching figure whose throbbing ambition is to employ the universal symbols to attract males bearing offerings of praise and libations. This fetish worship, so passionately encouraged by universal anxiety and commercialism, directly inhibits the risk of Mabel's settling for just one fetish worshipper. Marriage, to such a person, involves the risk of knowing and being known. The inability to run this risk accounts for family breakup and divorce increase on the part of those who discover first in the marriage relationship that fetish worship can thrive in the imagination, but never in reality. Divorce can ensue when the persons involved are first divorced from themselves, and each must reject the anxiety of knowing that the other as a real person is different than the figure created to serve the world of make-believe.

Only money can surpass sex in popularity, because those green coupons are redeemable in any situation to convert anyone into a fetish worshipper. We still insist that if Smith has more money, he somehow deserves more privileges and respect. And we all encourage this kind of worship to our own advantage, because we all stand a chance of amassing enough coupons to buy our way to the front of the pack.

Most of us are quite willing to settle on a very limited, but faithful, audience. Our friends say to us: "You're a great card player, Joe"; or "You're a great executive, Smith"; or "No one bakes like you, Mary." Where are the lies in these praises? No doubt in their implications. Can a person be anything? If he is a great card player or executive, who is the fellow who washes his face, drives his car, talks to his wife, and sits alone in a dark room? And who is Smith when he's not at the conference table? Who is that fellow who goes through the motions, and lives by waiting for the card table or the conference table? If Joe becomes a compulsive gambler, it is only because he insists on answering the question once and for all with a grand sweep of life's winnings. And if Smith does not soon find out who he really is, he will retire one day and wander around in a strange world. If all the world should faithfully read the teleprompter for the benefit of the actors on stage, they would still wander off to the dressing room and ask who the person was beneath the makeup.

Once persons ask these soul-searching questions in childhood and adolescence, they are not apt to ask them often thereafter. Men in later years are crucified to their own symbols of salvation. We have a work to do with the young people, but we find it distasteful because they too naively reveal our foibles and must be punished for their lack of subtlty in mirroring our sins.

Sydney J. Harris recently described some youngsters in a convertible: "Driving up to the country, I stopped in a little town for lunch, and took a table near the restaurant window. A white convertible drove by, with the top down; the occupants were two boys and a girl, all about 20.

"During the half-hour I sat there, they cruised by four or five times. They apparently had nothing to do and nowhere to go; what struck me most forcibly about them was their heightened awareness of themselves.

"Youth, of course, is the time for showing off—but this was a kind of public imitation of joy and happiness, as though it were more important to convince the spectators than to convince themselves.

" 'Look at us,' they seemed to be saying, 'young and gay and attractive in our new white convertible. Envy us, applaud us, make us bask in the radiance of your approval. We are having such a good time.'

"It all seemed so wistful and hollow to me. They were like marionettes, with no inner life of their own, who became animated only when public eyes were upon them. For their kind of intense self-consciousness is the deadly enemy of all spontaneity and genuine pleasure.

"But these have been among the paramount values of our society: the substitution of the 'image' for the reality, the taking of the shadow for the substance, the need to impress rather than the urge to express.

"The white convertible gave them a synthetic sense or identity that, by a cruel and familiar paradox, only served to blot out their individuality. . . .

"As we grow older, if our personalities are not allowed and encouraged to develop in creative channels, we give up our center of gravity in ourselves and transfer it to other people. Then, what they think, how they respond, becomes the tremendous measure of our content."

If the center of gravity can be transferred to others, imagine how quickly young persons, especially with their innate drive for venturesome self-surrender, may anxiously blunder into the embrace of sex or "love" as the most appealing fetish. Or human goodness! The more integrity and appeal our fetishes possess, the more we feel we have a right to demand the respect necessary to our wavering security. The line between greatness and supreme egotism often appears very thin indeed.

It seems we have no end of books which prescribe commandments to follow for salvation. We have easy helps to new self-confidence. These only encourage the dangerous business of reaching down into the soul with a chisel in order to carve out a splendid and appealing figure which the world, if it had its senses, ought certainly to adore.

Having done this, our struggles are often with our neighbors, who seem unfair with our masquerade roles. How easy to forget about our true condition when crusading for the responsibility of others to us. Wives don't bother to do anything about themselves so long as they consider their husbands "unfair." Here in America, his stirring campaign for equality and freedom has blurred the Negro's recognition that the primary obligation of bettering his condition rests on his own shoulders.

It is too easy to first determine what is coming to us, so that the obligations of maximum personal improvement devolve upon those who can influence us for good or ill. In tallying up what the world owes us, we have forgotten what we owe ourselves. When we realize our obligations to ourselves, then we can assess what we owe the world for *its* benefit, not necessarily *ours*. We all prefer the "other man" to make the first move; and the crusaders for a change in the world are often the last to change the world of their own making.

While it is true that it can be said of many of the world's

benefactors that they saved others, but themselves they could not save, it is also true that they never lost sight of the load of their own souls. Unless one first questions his own state, he is not of much value in understanding, much less bringing salvation to, another. Is a man's first responsibility to himself or to his neighbor? Paul would say that both go hand in hand: "Bear one another's burdens, and so fulfil the law of Christ" (GALATIANS 6:2). But lest our crusades to our neighbors be mixed with arbitrary requirements of what we assume is our salvation and therefore theirs, Paul adds, "But let each one test his own work . . . and not in his neighbor. For each man will have to bear his own load" (GALATIANS 6:4,5); and the "load" is self-examination first. Jesus was among a satellite people—they were harrassed and drifting like sheep without a shepherd. When a respected leader and minister to these people approached, Jesus told him, "You must be born again."

The burden of "buying" the responsibility of others to us and the bartering of our congeniality for theirs is a tiresome business. Take Hudson, for example. He is known as a neat, efficient junior executive. He has earned a reputation for hard work and a winning way with people. He is a great crowd pleaser. His fetish and the company's look identical.

Coming home from work at 5:30 p.m., Hudson undresses his personality. He feels that the whole world owns a piece of his soul, and he relishes going home to his "castle," where he can tell everyone on earth where to head in now that they have "bought a pound of his flesh" for a day's wages. He luxuriates for three hours in immobility before the TV, and woe to anyone who suggests he go somewhere, meet people, or start the old congenial bit again.

When Hudson is home he enjoys his liberty with a vengeance. Church is out of the question, because that means getting his good old urbane, happy-face mask out of the drawer and parading it around the pews in a sea of scrubbed and powdered faces. "No, sir!" he snorts. "We don't have to start that until Monday." Whenever Hudson sees a stream of happy, shining faces flowing out the church doors, he mutters, "Hypocrites!"

Hudson needed a good stimulus to give him the feeling of being alive. He'd try going out to enjoy himself, and would lose himself for months at a time in this sport or that hobby. After awhile he didn't enjoy anything if it didn't have some relationship to work and bettering his position. His wife commented proudly, "Hudson lives for his work."

Hudson sensed his emptiness and tried a self-improvement program. He tried reaching into himself and chiseling out a more perfect piece of humanity. He tried without success. There is just about nothing a man can do by himself, especially late in life, to change his basic personality.

Gregory Wilson puts his finger on the problem: " 'Suppose,' he [McElhaney] went on slowly, 'that what a man sincerely imagines to be his own deepest self turned out to be a pose. . . . I don't mean the outer self that the world sees, the way we see those shadows. I mean the inner self—the man we see when we look inside our own hearts, with all his ideals and fears and dreams. The man we whittle at and work with all our lives, certain that it's our true self we're whittling out. But if so, who's the whittler? How can we be sure we aren't whittling something false?' "

Hudson surmised, but never put into words, that he had neither the faith nor power to be his own whittler. The substance of the real man beyond the shadows and symbols was illusive, and he could never be sure that it, too, was not another mask, more subtle and deceptive than the rest. He concluded that his company's pronouncements of him as a success were more than enough for any man.

Hudson's near-collapse came one day when he was transferred and had to work closely with an expansive-vindictive neurotic personality. He was constantly being criticized, humiliated, and occasionally ignored by the new associate. The man was not simply an annoyance—he was a threat to Hudson's whole way of living. Hudson finally sought counseling. "If they don't fire this animal I'll lose my sanity," he moaned. "Either that or transfer me out of there. Just get me out of that department and I'll be OK."

Actually, meeting this fellow was the best break Hudson ever got. It was one of those wonderful troubles that come suddenly to shake the whole world of our making. Slowly he began to face his own reactions to this fellow. Why was he such a threat? What was he threatening? After about ten sessions of crying, "That fellow is a phony!" Hudson mumbled one night, "I wonder if he thinks I'm a phony, too. Sometimes I, too, wonder if I am."

Hudson might have been called "Nicodemus." This rabbi came to Jesus one night because Christ appeared as a crowd-pleaser that had to be won over. The rabbi, up in years, lonely and despairing despite his reputation, approached the Lord, flattering all the way. When Nicodemus paused, Jesus said, "You must be born again."

To have Christ pronounce the word "you" is a shattering experience. Men hear that word, and their hearts pound, they grope for balance. Men have always complained that their world did not honor their small gods. They have bemoaned their luck, their wives, their environment, their times, their inheritance; and matters for them have gone from bad to worse. What a shock that one of the first words God speaks should be "you": "Adam, where are you?" "You shall have no other gods before me."

When Nathan learned of David's adultery with Bathsheba, he fixed his eye on the king and cried, "You are the man." The word "you" fell like a blow on the heart. The word "you" is used eleven times in Nathan's indictment of fire in the *Revised Standard Version of the Bible*. The "arrows" of God found their mark.

The first step in becoming ourselves is accepting full responsibility for attempting to hide our nakedness with ventriloquism and crouching behind a masquerade role. The second is the step of surrender to Christ so that we may be reborn by faith through the power of the Holy Spirit. This *must* be by faith.

A woman took my suggestion that she come to me for counseling to understand her part in the failure of the marriage. When she told her husband that he ought to come also, he was outraged—he trembled with anger. Why so disturbed? Possibly the shame of owning up to his facade of self-rightness, based on his industry and honesty at the shop, was already an ominous feeling he did not care to explore. He was frightened at the possibility of appearing undressed, first before the whole universe, and then before himself.

If at the same time this husband were ever to recognize the

call to destroy his fetish, he would have to believe in Jesus Christ. If we are reborn by God's power, we are thereby admitting we do not have the power to remake ourselves. We cannot make ourselves into a new image. What shall we become? This is the daring leap of faith that keeps our eyes fixed on God in the fullness of His love. We do *not* know what we shall be or what we shall feel. We only know at the beginning that as we return to the image of God, we must reject the images of man. We must believe that we shall be fully satisfied with God and His power to remold us before we can be satisfied with ourselves and our own powers. The workmanship of God must take precedence over our workmanship. We must first be accepted by His power before we learn the power of acceptance.

We are reborn through Christ and by the Holy Spirit. Now what does this mean? It means that Christ restores us to our origins in the image of God. Our present lives are in time, but we have a destiny in the eternal God. We were created to be whole personalities to live in union with the holy God. All the images of the Old Testament refer to God in His holiness as "high and lifted up." This demolishes the modern heresies of Feuerbach ("theology is anthropology"), the Unity School ("God is my Power of Good"), and the antisupranaturalists ("God is the Ground of Ultimate Being"), and some of the ancient heresies, such as Vedanta ("the self is God —realize it"). Our individual selves are the offsprings of the sovereign Selfhood of the holy God, who is from everlasting to everlasting. We were created in the image of God, not God in the image of man.

Christ is the Image of God. God ". . . in these last days . . . has spoken to us by a Son, whom he appointed the heir of all things, through whom also he created the world. He reflects the glory of God and bears the very stamp of his nature, upholding the universe by his word of power" (HEBREWS 1:2,3). It is Christ who now restores the broken image. We are told to ". . . be renewed in the spirit of your minds, and put on the new nature, created after the likeness of God in true righteousness and holiness" (EPHESIANS 4:23,24). All men were destined to partake of Christ, who is the one Mediator between God and man.

Declares Martii Siirala: "It seems to me that finding oneself in an explicitly therapeutic encounter, or in one's life history as therapy, always means losing oneself into relatedness in two directions: first toward one's origins, often traditionally conceived as the very 'self-thing' in one or another limited system of reference; and secondly, toward something this origin can be fruitfully related with. In all of these directions—toward the past and the future, toward the local and the far off, toward the personal and the universal, toward man and toward woman—the selfness, as authenticity, or as being in the right place, or, theologically, as being a justified sinner before one's Creator, is not possession of our self but a share in Christ as the self of our self."

The power to explore and actualize our unique feelings and capacities is realized through personal wholeness and freedom exercised in loving relations with other persons. The Christ by whom the world was created and who restores us to the image of our Creator is, in the creative community of faith, the Holy Spirit. "Now the Lord is the Spirit, and where the Spirit of the Lord is, there is freedom. And we all, with unveiled face, beholding the glory of the Lord, are being changed into his likeness from one degree of glory to another; for this comes from the Lord who is the Spirit" (II CORINTHIANS 3:17,18).

Only the Christ who created our unique powers gives us the full confidence and ability to fulfill them through His Spirit in the relationship of love. And yet, fully honoring our freedom, we are exercising *our* powers and *our* capabilities and *our* judgment. When once God's holiness establishes the "infinite qualitative difference between God and man," then the Spirit of holiness becomes one with the spirit of the individual man. "But he who is united to the Lord becomes one spirit with him" (I CORINTHIANS 6:17). By investing ourselves through the Spirit in the eternal qualities of God, our particular deeds shine with an effulgence reflecting the glory of God's image.

Our spirits are divorced from His Spirit when we sin and fall short of this glory (ROMANS 3:23).

So richly and infinitely varied is the one God revealed in the individuality of every Christian that only through experience can one attest, "It is my spirit and the Holy Spirit working as one." In Ephesians 1:16,17 it is written: "I do not cease to give thanks for you, remembering you in my prayers, that the God of our Lord Jesus Christ, the Father of glory, may give you a spirit of wisdom and of revelation in the knowledge of him. The "spirit" in this case may be the teaching Spirit of God, or the spirit of man receiving this teaching.

Comments Francis W. Beare: "This ambiguity is often found in N.T. references to the Spirit; it points in its own way to the correlation between the Spirit of God, which reveals, and the spirit of man, which reaches out after and apprehends the revelation. The operations of the Spirit are not conducted within us as some force foreign to us, as in a spiritually inert or passive medium, but as in deep and vital integration with that which is most fundamental in our own personality, by the quickening of our own spirits in fellowship with and understanding of the divine."

The torment of fetish worship takes the life out of one. A man said to me, "I feel that life has knocked the stuffing out of me." His emptiness, however, was not due to life, but to its absence. We say he "lacks vigor, enthusiasm" (literally, "possessed by God"). He has no spirit. Nowadays we have shows, trinkets, and parties to "get into the spirit" of things. We horsewhip our tumultuous emotions to conform to our imaginings about ourselves and others, forgetting that whatever is flesh remains flesh, and the spirit of man can only be enthralled by these material crudities.

When we hope we can drink life out of a glass, we ask the liquor dealer for a "bottle of spirits." Getting one's spirit back is rather elusive when we try to buy a piece of life, wrap it up, and bring it home.

One is born into life. And the only life one can be born into is the sacred one created by God through Christ. When one is suppressed into spiritual insensibility, he must be reborn. God's life in us is dynamic, hopeful, enthusiastic; it is sacred; it is holy. If one wishes life, he must have it by the last Adam (Christ) who became a life-giving Spirit. The sinner must be born into joy by the Holy Spirit of Christ, for the true spirit of the sons of God is holy. That ". . . which is born of the Spirit is spirit" (JOHN 3:6), and "The spirit of man is the lamp of the Lord . . ." (PROVERBS 20:27). "Now we have received, not the spirit of the world, but the spirit which is of God; that we might know the things that are freely given to us of God" (I CORINTHIANS 2:12, KJV).

The Holy Spirit becomes one with our spirits, and infuses all our weak efforts with faith. God's love has been poured into our hearts by the Holy Spirit. Our hope in God will never turn to shame. True, the old cynicism about ourselves hangs as a sword over our heads: "Wretched man that I am! Who will deliver me from this body of death?" (ROMANS 7:24). The answer is that Christ, by whom nature itself was created, has the power to fully redeem creation. He has given us His Spirit as a guarantee that this redemption shall be completed in eternity (EPHESIANS 1:13,14; PHILIPPIANS 3:20,21; I PETER 1:3–9; ROMANS 8:9–25). The Spirit within us overcomes pain, fear, and death by the same might which raised Christ from the dead. This Christ who holds us by His own Spirit is Lord of our nature and is exalted Lord over ". . . all rule and authority and power and dominion, and above every name that is named, not only in this age but also in that which is to come" (EPHESIANS 1:21).

It is through this second birth into faith, not by the will of man, but by the will of God, that we discover how much there is to us. After this rebirth into the process of becoming whole and bringing our spirits into full conformity with His Spirit (sanctification), the subconscious is claimed for God. The child of hope becomes a partaker of "the divine nature" (II PETER 1:4). Then we know just how much power there is lying just below the surface! How many insights, how bubbling an enthusiasm, how potent a love, how viable a faith, how unquenchable a thirst for life! How thrilling of God to finish His creation! How persistent of God to take us for Himself that we may most forcefully be ourselves! How gracious of Him to receive us at our worst that He might use us at our best!

On Good Friday we sing the hymn "Just As I Am." It was more years ago than I care to remember that a young man of 17 stopped his bike near an outdoor church meeting while his friends went on ahead. The happiness of those young Christians, the message of the hymns, the sincerity of the speaker—all taunted my own discouragement by sharp contrast. Several months later I sat in the back of a church considering how I might refurbish my own favorite but tattered fetishes. The choir was singing:

> Just as I am, though tossed about
> With many a conflict, many a doubt,
> Fightings and fears within, without,
> O Lamb of God, I come, I come!

One is never so near hope as when he is suddenly struck by the futility of defending himself against the love of God. It is truly guilt which keeps the sinner from Christ. But once a shaft of light shines on the cross, that ray will broaden into the boulevard of heaven, where all the stars shine as beacons to our meeting with joy.

"You must be born again."

Yes, my Lord. Indeed, Thou gracious Christ. We cannot, we will not, resist Thee. Overcome us by tender power, by Thy mighty love. Breathe into the dust of our souls the breath of life again.

6

A New Focus on Life

SOMETHING HAPPENED TO me years ago that changed the world I was in. Some friends and I attended a concert. We were seated so high up in the balcony that I couldn't be sure I was in the right theater. The lad to my right kept up a running commentary on the singers, their dress, and the settings. I smiled, because I thought he was being sarcastic. No one could see much from our distance. For me, everything down there was a blur.

During intermission he fiddled with his glasses. I said, "I wonder what these do for me?" I put them on, and then I gasped. To my amazement, everything came into focus. He really could see the stage. I had needed glasses for years; but why bother going for an examination when you're positive you have 20-20 vision?

How are you seeing in your world? Some neighbors in my life view more and more for which to be grateful. "The rich get richer." But then again, "the poor get poorer." For others, nothing ever seems to go right. One can only surmise that the good Lord finds it difficult to bless some people. The astigmatism of anxiety and self-deception has so blurred the whole picture of God's goodness that only trouble-spots can be seen before the eyes.

When the world is out of focus, it becomes a hopeless matter looking for the right "detergent" to remove the spots. One can never be sure of the source or magnitude of the real difficulties. The real world comes to an end at the visual gate of our own pride. In Luke 1, Mary refers to "the proud in the imagination of their hearts." Pride is an imagined world; the real world is indistinct.

In his book *The Creative Years*, Reul Howe tells the story of a humble school teacher. She was directed to assist a class of dropouts and misfits. Her first problem was Joe, a fourteen-year-old who played the role of class comedian. At the crucial moment his best wisecracks would throw the class into hysterics. One afternoon the teacher kept Joe after school; she wanted to know why he wanted to make her life so miserable. He gave her a sullen look and answered, "Because you're such a sucker for it."

She sighed. "I know I am. I've always been afraid of people like you, and yet I'd like to be able to help you. Don't you want anyone to love or help you?"

The miserable fellow stared at her for a moment. Then he looked down at the floor and poured out the story of all his hate, poverty, and loneliness. Howe said, "Her honesty as a person called for the truth from this confused and resentful boy." This teacher accepted herself without pretense. She accepted this pretended comedian, and she enabled him to drop his pretensions and come to himself.

It is easy to take one look at ourselves, punish ourselves, and retreat to the act of false humility. God alone knows full well what we can be, and God alone has the infinite power to stand us on our feet and walk with us into a tomorrow of courage and persistence. But until the self is changed, the world stays pretty much the same.

Let's talk about Herb, a man who drove a meat truck through the southern states. When I first saw him, he was a coarse, uncouth, and cynical fellow; he drank heavily. He told me several times that he couldn't see Christianity at all—and no doubt he couldn't.

One afternoon I got an excited call: "Come over right away. It's my youngest girl. Polio. She isn't expected to live. If she does live, she'll be a cripple. It's hopeless."

I went to his house and spent an hour with him in his living room. "You'll have to pray for her," he announced.

"I'll have to *what?*" I asked. "Since when did you take to praying?"

He bristled. "Praying is your job. I guess everyone prays in trouble, though. I'll probably do some praying myself. This is a terrible time in my life. She is a beautiful girl. Nothing must happen to her. Nothing."

"Well," I assured him, "I promise to do some praying, too. It is my job. I like it, and I'm happy to do something so that no situation is ever hopeless. And I'm also happy that we'll both be praying. After all these years God will be very glad to make your acquaintance."

Four days later the girl got out of the hospital bed. The physicians shook their heads in disbelief. They assured each other that this wasn't possible, but, as a matter of fact, the girl returned home in a week without the slightest trace of the disease. Today she is a beautifully shaped young woman.

I stopped over to see Herb. "She might have gotten well anyway," I said.

He slumped in the chair. "Not to change the subject, but do you mind if I call you "Bob" instead of "Reverend"? That's all right, isn't it, Bob?"

I assured him it was OK, and we just sat there for a while. He didn't feel like saying too much.

"I suppose you think I should be in church now. Oh, I might surprise you some day. If I walked in, the church would fall down," he said.

"No worry. You're big enough to hold it up. Go ahead, surprise me. On the chance that somehow God reached over and touched your girl and made her well, tell Him 'thanks.' I think you might be the one to be surprised."

Herb was not a religious man, and most people aren't. His upbringing was pretty bad. He had been a golden-gloves boxing champ, and when he got too old to beat people up, he drove a huge truck, which gave him a sense of power. He drank heavily, because in his mind this signified vigorous manhood.

When he returned from worship the following Sunday, he collected all the liquor bottles in his house, paraded the family around to the backyard, and emptied them all. He never touched a drop of liquor after that.

Herb made calls on his friends, and after a bit we saw the most unlikely people walk into the sanctuary. He developed an enthusiastic devotion to prayer. For every problem his response would be the same, "Why don't we pray." Sometimes I thought he was "putting me on," but when he prayed aloud, it was with such simple sincerity that there was no doubt about his confidence in God to act on these conversations.

Herb was not a man to pretend. Rose-colored glasses are pride in technicolor. When we'd go to visit someone in the hospital, he'd tell me some sordid stories about himself. He felt that he had nothing to hide; and now that the past was behind him, he could look squarely into the future.

When we say that "the rich get richer," we mean that the open and grateful self is in touch with all the redeeming and health-giving forces of the cosmos, for all things were created through the agency of Christ. As gratitude increases, the person has more for which to be grateful.

One day my oldest boy, Paul, spilled a cleaning fluid containing powerful chemicals into his eyes. I called Herb, and we rushed Paul to the hospital. When the doctor finished bandaging his eyes, he could give me no guarantee that he would see again. It was a silent vigil at the hospital bed, and it was a quiet ride back home late that night.

The following Sunday, Herb and I were with the members of the men's Sunday morning Bible fellowship. After our study of the Bible, Herb suggested we pray for Paul. I remember the morning vividly. It was an electrifying experience. Because of my training in science, I have always been plagued with doubt. There is little in the faith I have not questioned, and sometimes the storms of confusion were more than I could bear. But on this occasion something was happening, and to deny it would have been materialistic obscurantism; to pretend it was all imaginary would have been pathological. The experience can best be described by saying that we were bathed in love and peace, and we felt extremely alive with a sense of disenthrallment. When we finished praying, each man said that he was overcome with a graphic experience of God.

A week later the bandages were removed from Paul's eyes. The eyes were healing. When the bandages were removed altogether, the physician stated that the healing was complete. He was a very kind and understanding doctor, who said on our last visit that this was a "miracle of miracles." I rushed over to Herb to tell him what the doctor had said. He pushed his fingers through Paul's hair and said, "Sure." Herb did his best to act nonchalant.

Gratitude makes us debtors to all mankind. The secret of such riches cannot be kept hidden. If the God-indwelt of this life love and serve their neighbors in the name of Christ, it is not because they have so many idle hours to fill—it is because they seek to ward off the embarrassment of *so much* divine love, *so much* goodness.

On those occasions when the routine gets so involved that we have difficulty keeping our head above the ocean of details, we then have added cause for thanking God for His church. Not all the goodness God has in store for me is going to come to me personally. It is our happy opportunity to share the goodness of others, and to thank God for the blessings which are ours because they have fallen upon those near and dear to us. There are times when the Christian is impelled to shout aloud his confidence: "Come all ye crucified with Christ! Sing for joy! Laugh in the presence of the grave! For you vessels of grace are herald's of God's conquest. Tell the whole world that the final word is 'love,' our destiny 'life'!"

Gratitude will never fully come into its rightful place until it is shared, expressed, revealed. Grateful men must do their work so that when any person wishes to find a way out of darkness, he can remember Jesus and be saved; through our living of the divine life, when someone asks, "Where art Thou, Lord?" the answer may come, "You have seen Him, and it is He who speaks to you."

The rich get richer. Take our grand and wonderful country, the United States of America. No nation in the history of man is as rich in wealth and spirit as is ours. Simply to be born here is inestimable good fortune. But millions of Americans live on the verge of emotional disaster. They persist in the hope that the welfare state, worshipping the "affluent society" god, will conduct them to the mecca of security and contentment. They are doomed to disillusionment. The gratitude that makes for peace is not an interminable inventory, it is exuberant satisfaction with life when, whatever our age, we greet it with the open heart of youth.

I can see this trait in my nine-year-old boy. Every sight, every sound, and every event are facts of extreme importance, moments of wonder. His heart is a "cup" that runs over. He took his first plane ride at six. The giant "bird" soared into the heavens. His eyes studied everything, his heart was attuned. To the dismay of the hostess, he stood up and exclaimed, "I could step right out on that cloud and shake hands with Jesus!"

The Apostle Paul had this kind of mind, because the power and care of God were his ultimate reality. In prison he said, ". . . for I have learned, in whatever state I am, to be content" (PHILIPPIANS 4:11). And again, "And whatever you do, in word or deed, do everything in the name of the Lord Jesus, giving thanks to God the Father through him" (COLOSSIANS 3:17).

The gift of knowing full well the divine nature of life itself is the gift of God Himself. While the happiness of so many people depends on forcing themselves to be grateful for the goodness of others, the happiness of the Christian is to be found in his gratitude for the goodness of God in the midst of all classes and conditions of men.

Thank God I'm alive!
That the skies are blue,
That a new day dawns
For me and for you.

The sunlight glistens
On field and on tree,
And the house wren sings
To his mate and to me;
The whole world glows
With a heavenly glee!

I know there are heart-aches,
A world full of strife,
But thank God, O thank God,
Thank God just for life.

—Ralph Spaulding Cushman

The salvation of life is our rapture, not because it is so vital that you and I should receive the gift of the eternal life, but because we, through this very life, can know the heights and depths of the love of God. If this be true, it has always seemed to me strange that some people find it necessary to see the dregs of society or the hopeless cases of a hospital clinic before they can be fully grateful to God.

Has the strangeness of a certain paradox ever struck you? For those who are divorced from life by the deceit of their own minds, the acts and thoughts of others determine their feelings, their very lives; on the other hand, for those who perceive the reality of life, there is a transcendance over the wounds inflicted by men and nature. Allen Gardiner provides an example. The anguish and sufferings of that missionary were unimaginable. As a witness in Patagonia, his life was subjected to continual crucifixion. At the end he was discovered on shore near a capsized boat. His diary was nearby, telling about the chronicle of pain and loneliness. The last words were feebly written in pencil "I am overwhelmed with a sense of the goodness of God."

Thankfulness is the work of faith on the mountaintop of living. Grateful souls see afar. They expect to hear a word from God in the tumult, to see the face of Christ amid surrounding shadows. And they expect to be saved by hope itself. Hope will not disappoint them, for the love of God has been poured into their hearts. Have you ever thought carefully of the words of Adelaide Proctor's great hymn?

My God, I thank Thee, who hast made
The earth so bright,
So full of splendor and of joy,
Beauty and light;
So many glorious things are here,
Noble and right.

I thank Thee, too, that Thou hast made
Joy to abound,
So many gentle thoughts and deeds
Circling us 'round,
That in the darkest spot of earth
Some love is found.

I thank Thee, Lord, that Thou hast kept
The best in store;
We have enough, yet not too much
To long for more;
A yearning for a deeper peace
Not known before.

How do we grow in gratefulness as a permanent condition of personality? By drinking in appreciatively the sights and sounds of truth and love which were unknown to us when our minds were previously fastened on our own images, defiantly pasted over the face of the world.

Word from the Prodigal

It isn't that the way back
Is any longer.
The mode of transportation is different.

Walking toward the father's house,
You see things you didn't notice
On galloping away.

—C. Moore Hunt

This disenthrallment, this detachment mentioned previously, is possible when one cultivates gratitude in prayer. The way some folks ride the bus or rush into the store, you would think each one carried the latest message to Garcia. But if one keeps at it, he can cultivate the habit of short prayers for commonplace blessings. The haggard looking man behind the counter, facing retirement; the self-conscious mother strolling behind the baby carriage; the busboy attempting to hurry with the dishes, under the watchful eye of the hostess; the utterly useless looking blind man to whom all passengers in the circle of a subway train would generously contribute, but who is ignored the rest of the time; the little fellow walking home from his first day at school, bursting with satisfaction; the new neighbor with the dark skin down the street, pretending not to care if anyone talks to her; and the faithful mailman—all of these people are very much a part of our lives, all searching in some way for life, all needing our prayers. No doubt this is why Jesus strides with such commanding leisure through the days of the New Testament: he notices so many people others passed by.

It sometimes seems so rude of God to stop us short, especially when we know He derives no pleasure from our afflictions. But looking out of a hospital window, or returning home from a meeting of prayer for a sick friend, one notices without sentimentality, but with deep emotion, some commonplace things which are more important to us than we realized. One is even surprised at himself some morning for thanking God for the rising sun, and not only for God's gift of the new day, but also for the faith to greet it. Yes, we pass through a world where goodness appears when we are ready to perceive it.

Being gratefully alert to God's goodness, we contribute to it and share it. In a famine we can say grace, and then fill the vessels in another's home with the oil of gladness, sharing what we have extravagantly, in the hope that when we return to our own home, our supply will be mysteriously replenished. There is no such thing as gratitude without caring. One can give without being grateful, but he cannot be grateful without giving. Blessings that are counted and hoarded are gone with the new morning. As Christ promised, "For to him who has will more be given; and from him who has not, even what he has will be taken away" (MARK 4:25). A disturbing fact! The rich get richer. . . .

A small boy was blind as the result of an accident shortly after birth. Every afternoon his mother would attempt to describe the beauty she saw. Little David would clutch his brown teddy bear with its one eye missing, and wonder if the sky and trees and water were as beautiful as his own mother.

An eye specialist invited the parents to his office, and said that he had discussed the case with a renowned doctor. They surmised that an extremely delicate operation might . . . well, it was a long shot, and if the parents did not want to get their hopes up. . . .

Their eyes brightened, for they had been told that his condition was hopeless. After several days they came to a decision: "Operate."

They all packed their bags (including the small brown teddy bear, along with other essential items), and on the way to the distant city they carefully explained to David that he must not be too disappointed if this didn't turn out the way they prayed. The parents were talking primarily to themselves, for youth is not too happy to reckon first with disappointment. In a short while he would be able to see for himself.

Several weeks after the operation, the bandages were slowly removed. Care was constant, and much patience was needed as the physicians continued assiduous treatment. Finally, the staff announced that the operation was far more successful than they had hoped. David could return home.

On the day of the trip back, Dave and the operating surgeon looked at each other in a hotel room, while Dave's folks stood by. The images before his eyes, blurred as they were, assured Dave that some day all the world would belong to him.

The parents discussed fees; they could not meet the cost at that time, but they assured the doctor that something could be worked out. He agreed. This arrangement, however, did not satisfy the patient. Pausing for a moment on the brink of an important decision, he suddenly reached for the teddy bear and thrust it into the doctor's arms. Father objected, but the doctor cleared his throat, pushed the toy up under his arm, and left.

Today in his luxurious office there is a silver-lined glass case. Mystified patients stare at the little brown teddy bear in the case, and read the words underneath: "This is the greatest fee I have ever received."

In a world where the decisions of a few are matters of life and death for the many, acts of kindness can seem as insignificant as toys. But gratitude insists on giving. God accepts the gifts. Our treasures are evaluated on His altar. And it is not the goodness which we can hold or share for which we are most deeply grateful—no, not those; rather, "Thanks be to God for his inexpressible gift!" (II CORINTHIANS 9:15).

In the final analysis, the gift to us of the Spirit of life in Christ merits from us worshipful praise, for being eternal, and returns to us the fact of our very being—this, the one possession which we can never lose.

Several years after I left Herb's church, I got word that he suffered a heart attack. I went to see him. A few months later he had attacks so severe that after his long recuperation he could not leave his chair to take more than two or three steps. When I saw him again, we both knew it would be for the last time in this life.

I thought of the cynical and rough man I had known a few

years earlier. Now I saw an elder in the church, a disciple who carried his certificate of membership on the seat of his truck to show his old buddies. We had gone fishing and hunting many times. He was a faithful friend.

I kidded him about his appetite, and he ribbed me about the time I got caught in a storm twenty feet from shore and couldn't row in. I started to speak once, and tears rushed to my eyes. As usual, he showed little emotion, but he preached a few of my sermons which I had forgotten. "You remember your own favorite passage, don't you? Romans 8?"

I nodded.

"You said once that with Christ the best is still ahead of us. Have you changed your mind?"

I assured him I still believed it. After a moment of silence, we both knew it was time for me to leave. "See you, Herb."

"See you, Bob."

Returning home, I knew he wanted me to think of Paul's symphony in Romans 8. The Apostle asks us what will be able to separate us from the love of God. He eliminates death first of all.

No, not even death.

7

My Friend Is Entitled to His Life

MY NEIGHBOR AND I need each other. In the expression of my self I need his forgiveness. James Michener said: "This is the journey that men make: to find themselves." That perilous journey is fraught with anxiety, trial, and error. It calls for convictions and decisions which are uniquely our own, and which will inevitably reveal basic differences between individuals. As the journey progresses, we revel not in friction of differences, but in the forgiveness which reveals our underlying unity. My friend must find his life in his relationships with me. He will succeed if I exercise the freedom of my own salvation, and if I make clear to him the assurance of God that he is entitled to his life.

While we say "entitled," we do not mean that this is obviously fair; rather, it is obviously faith. What seems fair does not always lead to the fruition of personality—it is this sense of "fairness" on our terms which withholds forgiveness and prevents our own souls from experiencing the forgiveness of God. The worlds of politics and economics are often played by the rules of "what's fair is fair"—my good turn calls for yours, and the opposite is then fair: Me? Forgive him? I'm paying for my sins. Let him pay for his." It is not too obvious that someone is entitled to his life when he has so flagrantly messed it up.

Throughout the New Testament God's forgiveness to us is

linked to our forgiveness of others. When we are gods to ourselves, we stand in omnipotent judgment on the people around us. Religion then has value principally in buying us a dab of forgiveness for our little foolishness, thoughtless mistakes, and the "petty pitfalls common to all us sinners." Our goal is "getting off the hook," the irritation with ourselves for making ourselves vulnerable in a world ruled by blind justice and personal scorecards. The problem of forgiveness for many people seems to be, "How do I get back into his good graces?" No doubt there are plenty of Biblical passages to remind us all that we are imperfect.

Gene Fowler tells of visiting W. C. Fields shortly before he died. The ailing star was sitting in the garden reading the Bible. "I'm looking for loopholes," Fields explained shyly.

God's heart was broken on Calvary, not because He was anxious about the inviolability of His law, but because, in the name of the law, men were jealous for the stunted conditon of their own selves. God was never in doubt about Himself. He knows what He has created and what each man is capable of being. He is preoccupied with our innate greatness, not our patent smallness. He is concerned not with proving that He is Judge, but, as Judge, bringing us to recognition of Christ as the fully divine Man. The Creator is not concerned with lifting us "off the hook," but, rather, with enlarging our capacity to share the divine Nature. He is dwelling on forgiveness not as the end, but as the beginning. His faith in our destiny to reveal the divine Nature is as inviolate as the law, which condemns us when we fail.

If we have not reached up for forgiveness in light of the whole plan of God for our lives, then we have not received forgiveness at all. In our modern theology, we have forgotten "forgiveness" as a legal transaction, and made it entirely a matter of progress in personal maturity. But the loss of the impact of the judicial aspect went hand in hand with a diminution of faith. Why deny it? The facts are on every hand. The world was created through the agency of Christ. Full revelation of the divine Nature is insured in every atom of creation. Fetish worship denies the rule of God, and man is in debt, with violations up over his soul. Our falling short of the glory of God cost us a penalty and penalized the completion of the entire race. The cross of Christ accurately demonstrates our violation, and both the cross and resurrection reveal God's determination that the victory of the divine Life must be the last word.

Repentance and forgiveness insure personal maturity when sin is viewed in the light of God's whole plan. You and I then see the exceeding sinfulness of sin.

The husband finds the courage to look into the eyes of the boy he has chastized beyond reason: "What a fool I was!"

The wife's eyes lift to those of the husband to whom she has been unfaithful: "What a fool I've been!"

"Who wants easy forgiveness?" stammered the young man in the pastor's office. "I can't get over the fact that it was in me to do such a thing."

Looking at ourselves from God's point of view, we are heartsick. True searching after forgiveness sweeps away all excuses. "Am I no further along than that? Is this all I have to show for forty years of living?"

Heartbroken.

The cross is the meeting place of dishonest people who are honestly heartbroken.

The only purpose of confessing all the sins one can remember is that one then comes to deal, not with isolated acts, but with the whole personality. One may need just a smile or a nod for one act; but for the whole self, why, for that one must be engulfed in a vast and depthless sea of grace, flooding the very core of being. No wonder the New Testament insists that truly forgiven persons must love the Lord God with their whole heart! To be forgiven for an isolated act makes us realize how basically good we are! To be forgiven because we are sinners through and through, however, makes us realize how utterly hopeless is our condition apart from the faith and power of God!

Jesus once told a story that carried the distinct "odor" of fire and brimstone, not because it mentioned "hell," but because it revealed both the patience and the uncompromising nature of God (MATTHEW 18:23–35). He said that a servant was brought to his creditor, the king. He owed his sovereign $10,000,000, and was told to pay.

This is quite a sum, prying open the imagination to grasp the enormity of our debt. No one disputes the greatness of the debt. The servant owes it; all know it.

There was no suggestion of settling out of court.

The man couldn't produce what was required. He asked for time. Time for what? What has he been doing with his time? He has nothing to show for $10,000,000? It took some time to work up that debt. Did the servant hope the king was a bit senile, and that perhaps he'd forget the whole matter?

"Mercy!" he cries. You could expect that cry, without seeing the script. "Show us, King, old fellow, that your heart is bigger than $10,000,000. I wasn't convinced when you entrusted me with that much. But now I'll be convinced if you forget it. Show how much you care for us subjects by cancelling the debt."

The king assured the subject that he has considered the plea for mercy. The servant assured the king that he would always be in his debt for far more than $10,000,000, and would be loyal to him till the end of time.

The king forgave the amount. The servant was swept off to freedom on a "sea" of forgiveness.

Did someone say he heard the fellow mutter under his breath: "If you knew I was bankrupt, why ask for the whole sum?"

Other nasty remarks are more audible. "If I am such a great sinner, why bother asking for perfection?"

"You mean I go to hell for not being a saint?"

"Well, I didn't ask to be born with all that potential. I would have been happy to be just a nice regular nobody."

"Come to think of it," said the servant a bit louder, "I didn't ask him for *that* much. Now he takes it out on me because he's so generous. I don't believe he was too fair about it."

"You'd think the King had more to worry about than the paltry debts of his subjects." Who made that last remark?

Speaking of "what's fair," one can also ask if the king had no right to his investment. If the servant knew it was borrowed for investment, did he think the monarch would never require a reckoning?

Perhaps no one would turn around and stare at our tattered condition with its makeshift patches if we didn't run through such wealth. No man ever sinned without paying a high price.

It wouldn't have been so bad if the human race had started at the bottom.

Anyway, some people don't feel too bad about that big debt to God. They have numerous other respectable deals on the "burner," and any time they want to they can take pride in those.

No, there was no question at all about the debt. At the time, everyone seems quite willing to receive all God is willing to give.

Young people are worried that they might miss out on the fabulous gift of romantic love. The trip to the altar, the vows for eternity, the wonder of the first child, and the happy new home—sure, these are God's gifts. "You might even say He owes these to us."

Several years later, perhaps several weeks later, there is some shouting, a few squabbles, and all the dishes are broken (you married people know how it is sometimes), and someone piously announces, "Maybe, I'm unworthy of your great love. Maybe we should not have been so quick to get married. It may be we're not worthy to be parents."

That's strange. Is there the implication that these ups and downs are days of reckoning? Does this mean it's too late *even in divorce* to say, "We're unworthy"? If all God's blessings were rented, the few would have it made, and the rest of us could start small, live small, and at the end declare an insignificant bankruptcy. Then we wouldn't need so much forgiveness. As it is, we thoroughly enjoy all the divine gifts, and we resent the stewardship, the care of money, family, talents, friends, and time, with God's investment in mind. Perhaps we just get this feeling in America, but why is it that the richer we get, the more we want something for nothing?

Some people say that a grateful person is a faithful one, but if so, that didn't include the servant of Matthew 18. He encountered a poor soul who owed him $20. Because of some misfortune, he didn't have it. The servant threw him in jail. The other servants were greatly distressed. We usually are when someone else isn't more forgiving.

What sort of brute is this fellow? How could he be so vengeful? Is he attempting to make a fool of the king? Possibly the king acted foolishly, but *he* would be more realistic (or materialistic, however you want to put it). This evil turn of events would have continued were it not that the king was still in charge, and the monarch had the servant delivered to the jailers.

The story ends with the ominous ring of a "buoy."

"So also my heavenly Father will do to every one of you, if you do not forgive your brother from your heart."

Does this story mean that God regrets the giving of gifts, or that His forgiveness is predicated upon mine?

No. An unpaid debt is a barrier. If it is forgiven, is it because the creditor is foolish? No. The creditor is gracious and the debtor receives grace.

This also means that honesty in recognition of debt is the prelude to a substantial relationship.

And this further means that it should be easier for a forgiven person to forgive. You cannot force someone to be gracious. The bonds of grace are stronger than the intention to pay an unpayable debt. Forgiveness is a risk—one sets the debtor free and gives him the right to go into debt again. Applying this logic to the Christian, gleefully playing creditor for every debt, real and imagined, should be rather distasteful to one who has been sued to the full extent of the law and found guilty, benefitted by full vicarious payment, and then been set free.

On the other hand, if one's real religion is fetishness, then he assumes—as do all selfish souls—that he is making a sincere try at this business of living. And, of course, it is no trouble to forgive himself, and play "god" with everyone who has injured him. In this case, he even finds it a struggle to forgive God!

Consider the case of Mr. J_____. He had, in two years, lost a beloved father, two sisters, and a son. He considered himself to be a religious man, and always found inner fortification for these bitter crises. He was quite close to his older sister. They enjoyed the closest rapport, and whenever the going became too tough, he could go to her and pour out his feelings, and she would understand. He once remarked, "When I am near her, it is like being near God. She is like a mother to me."

Mr. J——'s sister had a stroke, and then suffered complications. Her heart stopped, but she was revived. She lost her sight, her brain was damaged, she contracted pneumonia, and she suffered for two weeks in untold agony before she died.

Mr. J—— was torn by unremitting complaints. He fell apart. He could not forgive God for permitting his sister to suffer. He could not bear to enter a church. He could not listen to hymns on the radio. Life seemed pointless.

Through extensive counseling he came to see that he lived vicariously through the solid and gracious character of his sister. He deified her in order to make her responsible for his life. She was his true religion. The more he glorified her as a spiritual person, the more religious he seemed in his own eyes. Every night God must have slipped into her house to receive secret orders for the day. With her in charge, no problem was insuperable.

Mr. J—— felt quite omnipotent, without taking the consequences for himself. He unknowingly made grasping and unreasonable demands on others, although he considered himself generous. Whenever his gentle demands were not met, he was first furious. Others could sense his wrath when they didn't do what was in their best interests. He stayed angry with his daughter-in-law for five months because she married his son, and finally decided to be big enough to "forgive" her.

But he could not now find it in his heart to forgive God. Actually, on the basis he laid down, the Lord was not being fair. God had removed a god. If God is a jealous God, it is because He is jealous not only for His own glory, but also for the true glory of man.

It was extremely difficult for Mr. J—— to face up to his fallacious basis of living. As he did so, he said to the counselor, "Isn't it strange that I have considered myself so religious, and now I feel as though I am being converted. I am becoming a new person. The moment I saw I had to face life myself, I knew I could do it with God's help. It isn't until now that I've really wanted forgiveness. I want God to be God, and never to compromise with my illusions. I'm sorry my sister suffered at all. But I sense through my own present experience —somehow—that her suffering was a horrible thing to God."

God deals with us in Christ, loves us, forgives us, frees us. We love as Christ did and for His sake, we forgive, and through us the Spirit of life frees others. The soul of my neighbor cannot flower in the maturity of selfhood without my grace, and this grace is from God. If I withhold grace from another, I have withheld it from myself. One sins against God and himself, and if one is forgiven he is enabled to forgive others for what they have done. He is also able to ask their forgiveness for holding them guilty for what they did not do.

The forgiveness that not merely forgets the offense, but also seeks reconciliation for the offender, is the core of the phrase "from your heart."

I was at a mission service recently when a woman read a story from a devotional booklet. I smiled in disbelief. Thirteen years before that day I had heard the same story from a Korean student as he read a letter from home in the seminary chapel.

The Communists ravaged the town, broke into one store, and killed three sons before the father's eyes. Armies of the U.N. recaptured the town and brought prisoners to the city. The father identified the two soldiers who had killed his boys.

He pleaded with the authorities, and was granted permission to keep these North Koreans in his home, taking full responsibility for them. They stayed several years under the roof of this Christian, and learned forgiveness from his heart. We are almost repulsed at the thought of such forgiveness and meekness. The same feeling arises when we realize that God stood idly by while His Son was at the mercy of evil. But there is the catch! God was not standing idly by. The self-surrender of forgiveness radically changes everything. If the offer of forgiveness is rejected, there is suffering and one is made to look foolish, but God both strengthens and vindicates. If, however, the offer is accepted, there is suffering and repentance on the part of the offender, and a soul is reborn. Sin is costly, but the only other factor of comparable cost to cancel the debt is forgiveness; and unless the cost is paid, the world becomes unbearable for those who are living and those who are dying.

The two ex-soldiers entered a seminary in Korea to study for the ministry. Today both are a genuine credit to God's

Kingdom. As time goes on, many will trace their knowledge of the "good news" to the living and telling of it by one old man who felt that when he saw his sons murdered by soldiers, he had something in common with God.

In modern times we have witnessed an epic of forgiveness which cannot be matched in the annals of civilization. On the one hand, the U.S.S.R. exploited the conquered to make them satellites; on the other, the United States both labored and paid dearly for the restoration of Germany, Italy, and Japan. We have received former enemies back in partnership in the global task of building and guarding peace. The question of whether or not they would be grateful did not enter our minds at the time, and this is the basic test of "sincerity." The upbuilding of their social and economic life is sincerity's satisfaction.

Persisting in forgiveness is an ingrained trait in anyone who makes a daily genuine attempt to open his life to the Spirit of Christ in personal affairs. The maturity of us all depends on doing everything possible to help each man be himself, even when his personality, with its ambitions and opinions, is contrary to ours. William James once expressed a marvelous faith: "If you will believe well of your fellow men, you may create the good you believe in."

From time to time, someone asks me how he can help both himself and others by growing in the saving grace of a redeeming Personality. I would say that the first step is by making it easier for someone to forgive me when I have wronged him. That simply entails telling him I did wrong, and that I would be grateful if he helped me put the wrong behind us.

Secondly it is to my advantage to find less for which to forgive. What a blow it is to find even good people treasuring a grudge as if it were precious coin. Feeding smoldering resentment with gossip causes a conflagration. If Christ were with us in the flesh and spoke to us aloud, He would ask us how it is that some of us find so much needing our personal forgiveness. Van Wyck Brooks said, "How delightful is the company of generous people, who overlook trifles and keep their minds instinctively fixed on whatever is good and positive in the world about them." We can indeed discover slights to our ego if we continually search them out. As a matter of fact, with that attitude, we'll find more and more! But Montaigne had it right: "A wise man sees as much as he ought, not as much as he can."

We like to compare our fortune with that of the king's. Is it really as great as his? How do we figure that some persons got so indebted to us? An older member of the governing council of the city was not sure he could forgive a junior member for not recognizing his seniority and enlightened leadership. Here was a soul enmeshed in his little microworld, where, apparently very devoted to the council, he worshipped his leadership and imagined his indispensability. Whether or not the junior member could have been more considerate is not the question. From where the senior member sat, each debt was figured at $10,000,000!

Recently my attention was called to an usher who wondered if he could forgive someone's insults. The usher had been criticized for not following the chairman's instructions. Why should the usher forgive, especially when he has been slighted with a disdainful sniff and a wave of the hand? The criticism was deserved! Accepting the criticism kindly and perhaps even with expressed gratitude would have been an apt gesture of confidence in the critic. Sometimes it is impossible to tell the Lord we forgive someone, because in searching our hearts He would reveal to us that there was little requiring forgiveness.

Another step helping us to grow in grace is to pray for those who are guilty, even when we are the victims of a painful injustice. Whenever our course is confused, light arises when it is remembered that it is our ordained course to impart life to others as the Spirit of Christ has given it to us. Retribution cannot recover life. Justice will protect many, and it may be the means of confronting some with reality, but without forgiveness somewhere along the line, justice itself neither expiates the sin nor restores the guilty to life.

J. S. Mill once declared: "Lord, enlighten Thou our enemies . . . sharpen their wits, give acuteness to their perceptions, and clearness to their reasoning powers. We are in danger of their folly, not from their wisdom: their weakness is what fills us with apprehension, not their strength." Ingrained in that prayer for our enemies is the faith that once a man begins coming to himself, we can profit by his dealings with us.

It is also worth our time to commit Bible passages on the forgiveness of God to memory. Why? We must have the assurance that God has forgiven us for falling short of His glory. We must be able to forgive ourselves. We must help another human being to forgive himself so that his journey to selfhood in Christ is not detoured up some blind alley of self-recrimination. Once self-pity takes the place of forgiveness, life is constricted to a tight little cubicle, just big enough to store dusty, moldy old memories; outside is the open sky, but behind every "silver lining" one looks for big black clouds.

John Kord Lagemann tells us of Tom Anderson, whose existence was blighted by the memory of his part in a fraternity escapade that resulted in the death of a school chum. He went aimlessly from one job to another. After six years of marriage, he and his wife parted.

Rather suddenly the news about Tom changed. His wife returned. He was worthy of a fine position. One day he related his story.

"I used to think, 'Nothing can undo what I have done.' The thought of my guilt would stop me in the middle of a smile or a handshake. It put a wall between Betty and me. Then I had an unexpected visit from the person I dreaded most to see—the mother of the college classmate who died.

" 'Years ago,' she said, 'I found it in my heart, through prayer, to forgive you. Betty forgave you. So did your friends and employers.' She paused, and then said sternly, 'You are the one person who hasn't forgiven Tom Anderson. Who do you think you are to stand out against the people of this town and the Lord Almighty?'

"I looked into her eyes and found there a kind of permission to be the person I might have been if her boy had lived. For the first time in my adult life, I felt worthy to love and be loved."

We who hold in our hearts the divine love, hold there the divine power. We can punish or redeem. We can give life or take it.

We can build up or tear down, love or hate. We can play God and destroy ourselves, or we can trust God and gather life. We can mete out justice only and live under its punishment, or we can share grace and reap its peace.

We can live in the Spirit of life in Christ.

Or we can live alone.

The cross raised in the center of your personality is the symbol of life through travail. All those seeking life through forgiveness, and new hope through love, will be at home with you. We who cannot pay our debt to God will owe each other the love which made us brothers.

8

The Awesome Power Behind Humility

HUMILITY IS THE virtue supremely admired by Christ and most confusing to everyone else. It wears well on the strong, and is a token of fumbling in the weak.

While nothing may be so desirable as humility, nothing else is so indicative of the successful continuance of the greatest adventure in life—becoming truly ourselves in Christ. And without this venture, a striving for humility is not merely deceptive, it is positively disastrous.

"Acting humble" is a technique the proud individual apart from the Spirit of life in Christ has learned only too well. What is *really* going on inside of him? Modern science slowly catches up with the Bible. Originally we thought that the man apart from the Spirit of life sought *pleasure* above all; certainly, some superficial observations attest to the universal quest for the enjoyment of the moment. Then some schools of psychoanalysis insisted that the basic goal was *safety*; above all, they claimed, the anxious person wishes to be safe from fear, rejection, and disappointment. Is this the whole story?

Not by a long shot. The proud individual adopts his masquerade role early in life and impresses its alleged attributes over a select *circle* worshipping the same or similar fetishes in their microcosm. Obviously only an insane man advertises the worship of himself. We worship the false *image* or reflection of ourselves.

But, and this is an extremely important *but*—a fetish can only be a fetish if it is admired, worshipped, respected, and honored. Here we have it. Outside the Spirit of life, the prime motivation is not simply ease, isolation, or pleasure; it is the continuous longing for glory.

Jesus considered this longing as fundamental to an understanding of human nature. In John 5 Jesus said, "How can you believe, who receive glory from one another and do not seek the glory that comes from the only God?" (JOHN 5:44). Now the word to emphasize is "*only*." The quest for safety and satisfaction through glory is idolatry, the subtle worship of a false god.

Our personal glory depends on what others, for whatever reasons, grudgingly give. No one can buy fetish worship for his own gods without compounding his self-alienation by worshiping someone else's god. We find glory for personal gods by placating the gods of others—they buy us off, and we buy them off. So, then, one is morbidly dependent on the very persons he is separated from, he talks desperately at persons he is not listening to, he strongly needs persons he really does not care about, and he cries for help before the very persons whose fetishes he despises as frauds.

Here lies the essential difference with the neurotic. The neurotic person consciously knows no other person than the grandiose figure he appears to be. The selfish man who is not captured by severe neurotic trends knows that half the time he is pretending. He is married to his gods until death parts them, and he is married to the silly gods of his neighbors. Everyone comes into his fair share of glory by passing it around. "Humility" then becomes a bludgeon to beat others into submission. Flattery drags persons to our altars with rings through their noses. Catering to "the need to be appreciated" becomes a commercial enterprise of hoodwinking. Does it work? It *must* work. What a bitter pill it is to mix "appreciation" with so much secret cynicism, but in our time this seems about the only way to win persons over to our side! The chief complaint, however, is that our neighbors are all very fine people, but they tend to be ungrateful. "Why don't people reciprocate when we are so nice to them?"

The following is a letter typical of so many sent in to the popular "Dear Lovelorn" columnists:

Dear Ann Landers:

My husband never made much of a salary but we managed somehow. A few weeks ago I got tired of looking at threadbare carpets, faded curtains and a worn-out sofa. I went downtown and bought some lovely things on credit. I figured we'd pay for it somehow.

Sunday we invited a couple over because we wanted to show off our new things. These folks expect people to rave over every stick of furniture and every ashtray in their home. If you don't notice something they point it out.

Not one word was said about our new furnishings and I was furious. Will you please tell me why are people so mean?

SMILING ON THE OUTSIDE BUT BURNING ON THE INSIDE

The columnist's response was:

Dear Outside Inside:

Did it occur to you that perhaps they didn't notice?

Why are you so interested in impressing people you don't like? What a ridiculous waste of time and money.

The apt aspect of the letter is the characterization of the humility which didn't get a good return on its expensive investment: "smiling on the outside but burning on the inside."

It seems true, unfortunately, that outside of the God-given right to become ourselves, not every act can be taken at face value. Imagine! "Humility," the handmaid of "pride"!

Pride is protected when the little world of the microcosm is kept secure, the rules are obeyed, and there is fair play. The "self," then, is what we demand others see it as. Oscar Wilde once said: "Selfishness is not living as one wishes to live—it is asking others to live as one wishes to live." This means that I bring a script to the day's events, and I can be distraught when someone in the encompassing drama flubs his lines or misses his cues. Life can be regimented. My glory may depend entirely on the reactions, the smiles, the comments, the . . . well, every single act and word of those in the cast.

This poses an unbearable burden on being alive. The persons we trust become fewer and fewer. Tempers grow violent, because there are some people we'd like to tell off, but dare not. More and more we are found to be selling something. Writers write for writers. Parents at sandlot ball games for their youngsters are actually there for the adults. I notice that some ministers preach sermons only other ministers can understand or appreciate, and theologians talk almost exclusively to theologians. Because of this, we are all extremely sensitive. "Pride" is like a skin disease rubbed sore. If it is so much as brushed against by any foreign object, there is intense pain. The slightest compliment or sign of adulation becomes a matter of glory, even when some distant voice knows the whole truth of the matter. The most subtle sign of rejection becomes a matter of humiliation to which the proud person can never be fully inured.

This places "pleasure" in an odd position. Superficially, it is claimed that more persons are not Christian because they seek pleasure too much. Trapped in his own microcosm, it is unlikely that the proud person enjoys pleasure for its own sake. "Pleasure" is the twofold job of finding release from the noxious burdens of the existence-in-compartments and of establishing rapport with other members of the micrcosm—and usually these two functions merge. True happiness for him is a gilt-edged moment; it is a swift promise that glitters in a flash and becomes of greatest use to the luxuries of memory. Seeking pleasure becomes a job, a real grind, like daily voyages to the Siberian salt mines. The business of feeding nickels to the jukebox, perfecting the art of flirtation, parading in with another pitcher of brand new dry martinis, and reaching down into the muck and grabbing a laugh by the throat to bring it up reluctant is all a pool of stale perspiration. The biggest laugh is reserved for the act in which the overly buoyant comedian admits his foibles, and the humble-looking fellow gets hit in the face with a cream pie. No, "pleasure" is too big an item to be taken in a light vein. Too much is invested in it, and its laughs are too serious. To become a Christian might involve the person's admitting that he wasn't enjoying himself all that while, and too much is at stake to admit that, in exchange for what? Submission to a way in which the happiest are supposed to be the meek?

True pleasure may be spotted in children. It is a sad thing to see them lose both their buoyant humility and their ability to find pleasure at the same time. I sometimes wonder if the greatest problem the world faces is the dwarfing of every future generation by the forcing of children into foreign molds. Unable to resist consciously, they must embody emotions and reflect a moral pattern which are the products of our struggle against ourselves. Fifty percent of the discipline I witness today is savage, capricious, and a projection of our own hostility. We simply cannot tolerate the anxiety of watching the children exuberantly find pleasure "in nothing," make their own decisions, adopt their tastes, and realize their own talents. They grow up feeling that life is artificial, with artificial pleasures, and that their own feelings are of no consequence. Their search for a humble person to teach respect for authority, while loving and trusting them deeply, is best heard in the words of an old song:

> It's a Barnum and Bailey world,
>   It's as phony as it can be;
> But it wouldn't be make believe,
>   If you believed in me.

When increasingly we must find in existence solely what we *must* see and hear, only what we can afford to entertain about ourselves, the real world becomes narrowed to the dimensions of a pinhead. The senses literally become dulled, vision becomes tunneled, streets get narrower, breath gets shorter, ceilings get lower, people shrink, doors lock, details jam, time flies, existence drags, nothing envelops all, the sun dims, and night lengthens. After death the chief criticism souls will voice of the Scriptures is that hell was not pictured hot enough.

The nonrecognition of hell is one of the severest symptoms that one cannot behold life. Hell is the condition whereby the processes of death are hastening with accelerated progression. Hell is the torment of those who, in their own powers, could not disengage themselves from the glory of pride to flee to the integrity of the true life. Hell is the smokescreen of unreality bursting into eternal flames. Every moment, every observation only attests conclusively to this, that the alternative to life is hell, and in between is a narrow corridor where souls are hastening in either direction.

Jesus once said, "Truly I say to you, whoever does not receive the kingdom of God like a child shall not enter it" (MARK 10:15). This saving characteristic of the child is a grateful response to the loving and unquestioned authority of the parent. The child is convinced that love and power are unitive in guiding the young life, and his joyous confidence reflects his faith. If he becomes convinced that power is punitive and love is capricious, then he will defend himself against both power and love. He will eventually fall into the hell of something akin to the new *Soka Gakkai* religion of Japan, in which the adherents carry the *gohonzon* and recite from it frequently, "I am the supreme power." But in so saying he must placate all the powers of which he is secretly afraid and must defend himself against the love he so desperately needs but assumes will make him vulnerable; and he must depend upon, in some fashion of mock humility, all those before whom he loudly proclaims his independence.

Fears can only be magnified, for the protestations "I am the supreme power" or "I need no one because I've always made it on my own" only widen the chasm between oneself and the alleged enemies. In growing isolation the fears now emerge increasingly from one's own mind, and the remedy cannot be found in the real world. This mad cycle of fear and isolation is the unseen wall that stands as the pitiable pale of hell.

If, however, the person is saved back to life, it is because of the childlike faith that one cannot surmount the wall under one's own power. The divine love revealed in Christ must be accepted by faith at the same time the Spirit of life is lifting the personality over the wall into the glory of God. I take it this is one of the meanings of the old gospel song, "Love Lifted Me." In the real world the glory which comes from God is the restoration to one's true identity in the image of God, the return to one's sight, one's hearing, one's true emotions, and the integrity of one's self. This restoration is accomplished by the Spirit of life and through the ecstatic knowledge that one can walk directly into the frontiers of living, because for failure there is forgiveness, for humiliation there is grace, for impotence there is divine power, for alienation there is sonship, for wandering there is a Father, for human license there is sure guidance, for wounds there is healing, and in place of hell there is a haven of God, which is truly heaven.

This restoration requires childlike faith. But it is faith which demands obedience, for only in the real life can we see the glory of God in what He has made and in what He is.

My wife and I have covenanted with Christ and His church to give our boys Christ and His life. I have taken each of the boys aside on separate occasions and said to them, "Son, be open to life. See it, be committed to it, hear it, welcome it."

They are doing this. Last summer the oldest boy, (Paul, 11) and I were at Black Lake, N. Y., in a boat fishing. The bass weren't biting, and we had only half an hour before complete darkness. My surface plug was shooting toward shore like clockwork. All the while the boy was mumbling something. With a good deal of irritation I growled, "Why don't you get to work on these bass, instead of talking to yourself as if you had lost your senses."

As my plug shot out again, he persisted, "Ah, now it's perfect, just perfect." I looked up and understood—the lake looked like glass, the sun was bathing the western sky in pure fire, and the clouds hung motionless like colossal works of solid marble gleaming red and gold, a string of ducks were crossing the lake, and the open flowers of the lily pads were rich in the autumn of the day. The boy and I sat together in a quiet and reverent bond, feeling that we had a vital place in the eternal and kind wisdom of God. I smiled as I remembered accusing him of losing his senses. He had full use of his, while in my frustration at the poor fishing I was losing mine!

Now we approach true life—this is, in increasing gratitude to God, to be open and teachable before life, so that the false self enclosed in the microcosm dies and the true self emerges as a soul free from hell, from unreality, and from the wicked phantoms of imagined fears.

"Being teachable" means that one learns of Christ in all of life—one is a disciple. The *New English Bible* translates John 1:4 thus: "All that came to be was alive with his life, and that life was the light of men." The disciple is humble before the face of Christ on the universe. Said the poet:

> I see His blood upon the rose
> And in the stars the glory of His eyes,
> His Body gleams amid eternal snows,
> His tears fall from the skies.
>
> I see His face in every flower;
> The thunder and the singing of the birds
> Are but His voice—and carven by His power
> Rocks are His written words.

All pathways by His feet are worn,
His strong heart stirs the ever-beating sea,
His crown of thorns is twined with every thorn,
His cross is every tree.

—Joseph Mary Plunkett

All things that in the fulness of time shall be united in Christ have an instinctive gravity toward His rule. The thunders of history's storms are the crashing hammers of God forging His purposes on the anvil of His Word in the fires of our defeats and our victories. The Spirit of life deciphers living for the humble disciple who sees in every struggle a sign of God calling men from enslavement to freedom. In the seed is written the will of God that a leaf shall drink in the sun and a flower shall bloom. The disciple, because life flows widely through His soul, is horrified at the disease which blights the rose and the sin which blackens the spirit; but He trusts the ability of God to do His will. It is the will of God that man and earth flower under Christ, the Sun of righteousness.

The "ultimate truth" is not simply what appears to be, but what God can bring to pass. It demands training to look at an enemy and see His friendship. It demands discipline to observe pride and see also His proffered grace. God cannot share our pessimism, for behind every hand uplifted with a stone of cursing, there is the heart of a great apostle willing to preach the gospel of love to every soul.

Whose heart will change today? What fists, closed in hate, will open in love? We work confidently in hope. We wait humbly in faith. No one fully knows what God can do, but one who has humility is ready to be startled. All of Christ's life, including His death and resurrection, is His promise that the humble will not be disappointed.

"Humility" is nourished on hope. Sentimental and wishful thinking are dashed on the rocks of disappointment, but hope is rugged. One who has hope can be bruised, disappointed, and discarded as a dream; and yet he forges into tomorrow with eyes open, with mighty prayers ascending, and with heart listening. God is at work. If God can forsake us, then "humility" can abandon "hope," but not before.

How could we define "humility"? It is a hopeful and grateful response to the integrity of life—it is not impressing, but expressing one's being in faith; it is acquiescence in the right of others to express themselves as they see their purposes; it is the giving of freedom to other men to live and be themselves, not judging them when they seem to us to fail, encouraging them by faith when they permit us.

"Humility" lives—it is wide-eyed before the wonder of Christ in all that He has made and in every heart that He is working; it tears down every barrier, sees every frustration as an opportunity to learn, and requires the grace of God as a thirsty man longs for water lest he perish in the wastes of defensive pride and vainglory.

While I personally cherish my friends, I have learned much from my enemies. They have showed me where the fires of pride were not yet banked in my heart, and how the best of human judgments can be a cloak for one's own need to be right at all costs. It is surprising how much truth one can learn if he is willing to pray for his enemies so that he can listen to them. The Christian seems often to be taken in, but if he must, he would rather be taken in by others than by himself.

"Humility" is being open first before God, then ourselves, then others. The secret of patience with others is usually in understanding ourselves; this is especially true in marriage.

A married couple came to see me. This was the second marriage for each, and now they were contemplating divorce. I suggested that they work from the angle of humility.

"And let him walk all over me?" the woman asked.

"It all depends on what you mean by being humble. Humility involves a deep respect for the freedom and dignity of others as God's creations."

"Who could respect *her*?" the man sulked. "Why just yesterday. . . ." And on he ranted.

"Let's face it," I said. "You don't know each other because you can't face yourselves. You project your feelings on to each other and point the finger of blame for what you don't like in yourselves. For example, Joe, you were always taught to be methodical, precise, expert. When things go wrong at work, you enter the house roaring that it is upset. Helen, you are becoming anxious now that your daughter is in adolescence, so you nag Joe for not taking a greater interest in the children."

"If I said nothing," she rejoined, "he'd never think about it."

"No," I said, "not in this frame of mind. But you don't know what he can do. You can't even *see* him because you are locked up in your own anxiety. Each person in this marriage must think of the problem in terms of himself. Before you berate the other, ask why you don't like it. You can't ask the partner to be responsible for problems you can't handle in yourself. The salvation of marriage begins with the salvation of its individuals. When each brings himself to God for testing of himself, he will find the resources of life bubbling up from within him, without demanding the other be responsible for his own lack. The intimate union of marriage requires trust and independence. When you say 'I require you to . . .' you usually mean there is something about yourself you can't handle. The person who says, 'I don't have any confidence in my partner,' must ask, 'How confident have I been of myself?' "

Joe was the first to discover that when he listens carefully and courteously to Helen's complaint, she is enabled to see how she has projected her own anxiety into the problem. These two people are successfully working at their marriage from a new angle, and I stress the word "working."

When we glimpse the awesome power of humility, we see that it is not a lame and apologetic "knocking on life's back door." It is an heroic, almost senselessly intrepid crusade for principle and God into which the soul has been lavishly poured to the last atom. "Humility" is God's clever method of confounding the wise and confusing the strong—open to all of life and its needs, the truly humble is committed heart and soul to purpose; seeming to be the servant of all, his self is ennobled; losing his self to the whole world, he inherits the earth.

No one but the meek person can afford to be himself. Ralph Waldo Emerson said, "Insist on yourself; never imitate. Your own gift you can present every moment with the cumulative force of a whole life's cultivation: but of the adopted talent of another you have only an extemporaneous half possession." The more open to life the humble man is, the more he is able to nourish the power of his own gifts. He can be certain without a closed mind, and he can be positive without arrogance. The whole world can feel his full impact without having to contend with the debilitating disease of "selfishness." As it is written in the Scriptures, "But let each one test his own work, and then his reason to boast will be in himself alone and not in his neighbor" (GALATIANS 6:4).

It is thus that one's pride is always shocked by the unshakable confidence of the meek. A proud person feels that some trick has been played. The Pharisees disposed of the ragged fanatic from the hills, John the Baptist. Pride wondered why it did not turn off the volcano with a snap of the fingers.

Paul himself had to admit that his enemies were partially right. Without the awesome power of the Spirit of life in Christ at home in his spirit, he was, as they said, not much of a stammering little Jew. By his humility he was indeed so convincing that a part of Christendom claimed it was founded on Peter; it bypassed the prince of Apostles, the statesman-missionary of the Gospel.

When the soul knows itself, it often becomes the object of ridicule by those who cannot comprehend unpretentious behavior. Some of us remember Mayor Fiorello H. LaGuardia of New York City. He lived for the sprawling city as though it were his own sweetheart. Five-alarm fires found him at intersections directing traffic. You did not find then the vile filth on the newsstands and in almost every bookstore and drugstore that you find today. Corruption lived a short life under his boisterous reign. When the newspaper workers went on strike, he spoke on the radio and read the comics to the young at heart. Colorful, dynamic man that he was, he once remarked, "When I make a mistake, it's a beaut."

To be free from the tyrannical illusions of the false self is indeed to be invigorated and in love with life. What a glorious paradox! To be free of self and master of self at the same moment!

One afternoon Toscanini worked with his musicians in producing the *Ninth Symphony* of Beethoven. He was such a master of interpretative feeling, that suddenly these professional men got to their feet and began applauding. They stamped, whistled, and clapped, while the master stared first in surprise, then with a frown. He waved his arms for them to be quiet, and, with tears streaming down his face, shouted, "Gentlemen, it is not Toscanini. It is Beethoven."

It is not possible to ignore the identification of the truly humble with Christ. The diseases of deception constantly assault the humble. In support of those who are dependent upon God, the Scriptures provide great promises for aid. The false faces of fear are the guises of time, but are unavailing before God's purposes in eternity: "For lo, those who are far from thee shall perish; thou dost put an end to those who are false to thee" (PSALM 73:27).

This being true, once the true self is in expression, there is no need to lie down and slowly die of anxiety. When Jesus told us to turn the other cheek and to forgive seventy times seven, he was delivering a mortal blow to the ramparts of pride's cardboard castle. Armed with the power and purposes of God, Christ expects His people to struggle until weary, to fight hard, to pray without ceasing. He expects you to know full well when vindictiveness seeks to prostitute your good will. When the mob was going to stone Jesus, he walked defiantly through them; but when they came for him in the garden, he went as the Man of Sorrows. There is a time to stand on your feet and fight and a time to be crucified for what is right, and only those in possession of their souls can be trusted to know the times.

Humility causes us to trust God and have no fear of pain; to stand with God to cry to the children, "Grow strong in light"; to cry to friends, "Be yourself that I might know you, and you can trust me to give you courage"; to smile at the self, laugh heartily in the joys of being alive, but enjoy only the humor that buoys and never stultifies; to cry to strong and weak alike, "I see you struggle for your destiny. Let us walk together with Christ that we may succeed."

And when there is none near in the hardest hour, and, in your slipping, you—like all true prophets before you—wonder at the success of the wicked and the ease of the proud, throw the torch to God, who shall give it to the man now ready to follow in your steps. Above all, let your servanthood call for God's "*therefore.*" The world was made through Christ. He who cast stars into the heavens and put a torch to the sun gave His back to the smiters. The earth's beauty is but the fancy of His mind, yet a crown of thorns was thrust onto His brow, and the blood trickled down His face. He humbled Himself and suffered death on a cross. *Therefore!*

"Therefore God has highly exalted him and bestowed on him the name which is above every name, that at the name of Jesus every knee should bow, in heaven and on earth and under the earth, and every tongue confess that Jesus Christ is Lord, to the glory of God the Father" (PHILIPPIANS 2:9–11).

If that be true, there is no need to "throttle" life.

> O Lord and Master of us all
> Whate'er our name or sign,
> We own Thy sway, we hear Thy call,
> We test our lives by Thine.

The fever of life is cured.

The storms of frustration are settled.

The petty struggles of bantam tyrants are being canceled by peace.

He who was humble is Lord of all, and the servant is not greater than his Lord.

9

Hypnotized by a Mountain

MOUNTAINS—INESCAPABLE AND seemingly defiant—have always fascinated man. Their grandeur makes him reverent; their height has taunted him; their mammoth arrogance is a fit challenge for God to tunnel through ("Got any mountains you can't tunnel through? God specializes in things thought impossible . . .") or to remove altogether ("Be taken up and cast into the sea . . ." (MARK 11:23)); their terrors of cold and uncut face beckon man to assault them as an offering to God. In an age when he is becoming the servant of finicky machines, man loves to engage mountains with his bare hands.

The thing which "might be done" for many and "must be done" for the man of faith in God looms up tauntingly like a mountain. It becomes a landmark around which life revolves, like the mountains easily seen by a newcomer to Denver, telling him it's just a matter of time till he goes to meet them.

To Jesus the mountains, which symbolized His mission, magnetized Him to prepare for his crises.

Christ stared at the large, the looming, the defiant goal, and wherever He went, He knew His steps took Him closer to "my hour." The decisive "battle" of Mount Calvary was not decided in the Garden, but on a mountain in the beginning with Satan when Jesus stared into the will of God and decided that the world was going to be won for God by His methods and none other.

The central great goal of a man's decisive hour is one he broods over, knowing it is in His mind, too, and no matter how he wishes, waits, ponders, or procrastinates, it will not fade away. In the morning there is no use looking—it will still be there.

Two things keep you from your mountain: the first is imposing piles of routine tasks, clamoring with an incessant tinny urgency; the second is fear.

Fear darts out of the shadows in familiar costumes: fear of failure, ridicule, loneliness, physical injury, poverty, death. Fear grows once obeyed.

Since fear was created for man's benefit, it becomes a dreaded enemy when we run from it. Running wildly, it seeks homage in the darkest and silliest retreats of the mind and can attach itself to the most innocent things. It needs to be tamed, stared at, questioned, examined, probed, and pinched.

Once tamed, fear becomes an ally. It is the steed upon which courage rides to its battle.

Fear is a tool of conscience—it is rare energy equipping us to meet a great foe. "In the days of his flesh, Jesus offered up prayers and supplications, with loud cries and tears, to him who was able to save him from death, and he was heard for his godly fear" (HEBREWS 5:7).

Once having encountered his fears, man cannot be the same until he has either assaulted the mountain or turned back.

The real mountain—the loftiest—is the will of God specifically for your life, which can only be done through love and persistent obedience. True cowardice substitutes a gallant preoccupation with molehills. The haughty rightness of America's Black Muslims or Europe's neo-Fascists is a thrilling charge on a pile of beans: the restoration of beaten pride.

If nothing less than Christ's plan for your life is the true goal, then let the seeming impossibility of it cause great fear. The very living and dying in faith is salvation. Cowardice is not surrender to fear—it is surrender to no-God; it is the screaming creed that the final truth is the enormity of sin, that what an indifferent crowd does not want to do is not worth doing, and that what is too hard for man is impossible with God. "He who conquers shall have this heritage, and I will be his God and he shall be my son. But as for the cowardly . . ." (REVELATION 21:7,8).

Faith begins with reality. A man of faith faces the reality of the hardest and best and makes an ally of it. Faith grows, like a mustard seed, until one might say with conviction: "Very well, then. There is a mountain." It may do nothing more, but with faith man has taken the most vital step in maintaining integrity: facing the truth.

Once you are reborn by faith in the Christ, there is usually very little difference between the will of God and what you want to do at the deepest level of your being. That may shock you. Probably because of our morbid misunderstanding of original sin as a virus infection of the chromosomes, instead of separation from the Holy Spirit since our birth. The truth is that God equipped us by birth and training for our purpose in the world.

You are on the most solid ground when a life of devoted prayer brings you into conscious touch with the deepest undisguised longings of your personality: "Therefore I tell you, whatever you ask in prayer, believe that you receive it, and you will" (MARK 11:24). Faith and love work hand in hand in exploring these longings; that is why there is always a condition attached to Jesus' remarkable statements on prayer (MARK 11:25).

Jack came to see me every Monday night shortly after he started worshipping God. He was afraid of everything, but especially his wife and mother-in-law. Now his plant was closing, and he was being dismissed from his job. "I don't know what to do," he muttered. He was getting physically ill, and grew worse when he found himself without a job and with little self-esteem.

One night I asked him, "Tell me, Jack, what would you really like to do more than anything else?"

"Be a respectable citizen who can stand on his own two feet," he said.

"I know. But for your work."

A slight smile tried to break through; it disappeared. "Oh well," he said, "What's the use? My wife would laugh. I'd end up a total failure. There's no use in talking."

"But it's just you and me, so go ahead and tell me. We have lots of time."

I thought he was going to say something like "I'd like to open a gambling casino in Las Vegas," but instead the smile returned and he said, "I'd like to be in aluminum."

"Oh," I replied, a little mystified. "The stuff they make pots out of?"

"Pots!" He half raised out of the chair. "Everything will some day be made out of aluminum. Let me tell you about its properties. It's uncanny. They'll be making tractor motors, engines, whole houses out of it, and that's just the beginning."

"Is that right?" I asked good naturedly. "A whole house, eh?"

"Right. And if I had a store, I could sell siding, awnings, railing, then branch out, and then. . . ." Half an hour later he was still spellbinding me on the romance of aluminum.

Every Monday for a month or so we just sat and stared out of the window of his mind at a great mountain of solid aluminum.

One Monday he breezed into the office a little wild-eyed, like a man who has committed the perfect crime.

"What happened to you?" I asked.

"I rented a store. I contacted my suppliers. I have a salesman to work with me. I'm taking a mortgage on the house. My wife will hit the ceiling. The first year will be rough." And on and on he droned.

I believe he was so afraid, he couldn't sit still. But that was a couple of years ago. The last time I saw him he was planning a trip with a loving wife (he didn't mention his mother-in-law) on his yacht on the Ohio River. He has a handsome business. And, incidentally, since his counseling days, a friend of mine has started work on tractor engines made of aluminum, and a nearby plant is manufacturing whole houses out of it. Great stuff.

People were born to have faith like fish need water. Face the truth long enough, and it is inevitable that you will act on it, either starting toward it or running from it. Keep your eyes on the man brooding over the truth.

Read tomorrow's history in the eyes of one who is not so much free from fear as possessed of the notion that with God it's not a question of possibility, but a matter of time.

No one paid much attention to Dr. Martin Luther King brooding about the necessity of desegregating public buses. No one knows how long he just sat and stared at the mountain.

When Jim Whittaker thought about climbing to the top of Mount Everest, 29,028 ft. above sea level, only two expeditions had made it before him. He said to his wife, "I'll be as happy to go as high as I can or as high as I am permitted to go—either one." By the time of the expedition, his attitude was a bit different. Psychologists asked the team if they would make it; some answered "I hope so" and others "I'll do my best"; said Jim Whittaker, "Yes, I will." May 1, 1963, he made it; and once the first American had succeeded, that very same month four other Americans followed his steps to the top.

In our church when we have a difficult task to be done, we call the person we feel the Holy Spirit has led us to and say, "Study this task with us. Think about it. Pray that it will succeed. How would you handle it?" Sooner or later there is a call: "Do you have anyone yet?"

Once the die is cast and the course set, fear becomes a great friend. I. A. R. Wylie said that he traveled to Britain during the impossible days of the air bombardment, and found the people keyed up by fear to heroic acts and extraordinary keenness. They had exhibited superhuman capabilities. "Some persons—explorers, adventurers, mountain climbers—are fully conscious of this power of fear to release them from their ordinary limitations. Ostensibly they may seek scientific data. But basically they are seeking the joy which comes to us when we have surpassed our normal selves."

We must admit that many of us see this, and can go no further. When the mind begins to race in circles, the palms get sweaty, the stomach churns, and the heart pounds; one thought screams—"Run away!" What assurance do we have that we can take these turbulent feelings and press on?

While for many, Christ leads to the truth, for some the truth once explored leads unmistakenly to Christ. The power of the Creator and Father of Jesus is granted to those committed to the truth wherever it leads.

The cross is the symbol of the Christian mountain for the Christian man. He broods before it in worship because he is crucified to it in life. It is both stark reminder and incredible joy that redemption is born of the marriage of truth and suffering.

The charge that the church is filled with people who do not follow what they profess is readily admitted. The church is a body of people who say that no matter how anxious they are about the knowledge of themselves and their neighbor's sins, the grace of God permits—no!—*constrains* them to still stare into the truth. The forgiveness which preserves honesty is the only island of integrity in a vast sea of degradation. The true faith is jubilation at God's patience and an undying trust that if we worship the Truth, sooner or later He will give us strength. Admittedly it is a faith, but the Bible confidently expects that in the day of judgment, Christians can be judged by the works of faith, rather than by the words of a creed.

Temerity stumbles into timidity when the truth is not clear. In a mountain chain of perplexity, is the peak before me the right peak? Is it God's will that I climb it today? How?

It may be too late to ask, "What is truth?" when suddenly facing a cross. After a tortuous life of deceit and compromise, Pilate probably did not know.

Every self-disciplined obedience to the moment's light builds the fiber of courage for life's decisive struggles. Or struggle. To most, every stormy event is a sudden annoyance to be resolved or escaped; to the Christian man, it is God's gauge taking the maximum measure of the total life, the depth of faith.

Life is mostly froth and bubble;
Two things stand like stone:
Kindness in another's trouble
Courage in our own.

—Adam Lindsay Gordon

Every spark of light struck from a courageous decision will one day burst at once in that inner shining that men call a "hunch" and the Bible calls "knowledge." The grace of God trains us (TITUS 2:11,12). Suddenly called to do the "impossible," our ascent will be unmixed with the fears of ridicule and disgrace which cripple those who want to climb before they walk.

Scotland's Eric Liddell, Olympic track star, was world-famous for running the 100-meter race. At the 1924 Olympic games in Paris, France, the air buzzed with stories of his training and power. There was no doubt he would win.

Liddell was dumbfounded when he heard that the 100-meter

dash was set for Sunday. A devout and sincere disciple of the Lord Jesus, he firmly believed that the Lord's Day should be one of rest and holiness—Olympic games were out. Right or wrong, it is still true that one's convictions are worth only the courage it takes to stand by them before the world. He said, "No, I cannot run. God would not be honored if I failed to keep His day." He was ridiculed.

Later he heard that a runner was needed in the 400-meter race to replace a man who had to drop out. Would Liddell substitute? This called for different training, but he volunteered.

At one point in the race he was bumped off the track and was 20 yards behind. Uncanny resources rescued him, and he sprinted ahead to win and set a world record of 47.6 seconds.

The time came when Eric Liddell served God as a missionary in China. When he faced his severest test, his convictions about life never wavered and he died in a war camp. To those who knew and loved him, it was clear he was moving up the slopes of a mission so Christ-centered that its peak could only be a spire in heaven itself.

When the soul is pure and your short life is counting heavily for God, don't you sense gloriously that there is no defeat? . . . that there is no death?

Do you not, in exultant prayer, thank God for what other people discover only in heaven—that it is all true, and that fear is a friend of life, not death?

Brood before a high mountain. When He listens, pray. When He calls, answer. And when you are ready, rise up and move toward it.

10

Sound of the Bugle

IT IS STRANGE how appearances become so deceptive that the truth feels like a wallflower at the evening's festivities. Let's look at a man who passes the church and is grateful he has no need for it. He has the notion that it seeks to change all his comfortable ways and make him into something he is not and was never intended to be. If by accident he reads the New Testament, he thinks, "If Christ came to give me life, what on earth am I living now?"

Engrossed as he is in this world, it can only come as revelation that this life is sacred. God gave us life, and life as it is revealed in Christ and imparted by His Spirit is not a foreign strait jacket. It is to be known, enjoyed, and lived here and now in all its wonder and inspiration. *This* is the life, to be known in its fullness by each individual personally. Through all its sorrows, joys, hardships, and victories, despite sin, and beyond the weight of finite circumstance, *this* is the life.

As we have seen, when man takes the center of gravity from himself and places it in the center of a microcosm; when he says to his neighbor, to his friend, his family, his job, "This is the image of me, now glorify it!"—he becomes devoutly bound to matters of duty. "It becomes your duty to live my life as I see fit. And it becomes my duty, in return, to live as you see fit."

It is no wonder that duty has come on hard times. It has always been misunderstood by so-called "devout" people. As soon as you speak of the self-fulfillment of the individual as the "will of God," you are accused of Freudian anarchy: "Ha!

This heretic is telling us to do what comes 'natcherly,' and we'll all end up God-blessed, self-indulged pumpkins. Anything that has to do with God should smack of medicine, discipline, rigorous self-abnegation, and, above all, *duty*!"

It is a wonder how any of us can go wrong, with everyone telling us our duty. It is certainly not beyond duty to try a little blackmail if the need calls for it. If it becomes my bounden duty to solve your problems as I see them, how can you evade the duty of solving my problems? Heaven help the downtrodden, who are the victims of every floundering Quixote's religious duty!

By contrast, we see the history of the church studded with human gems who sacrificed time, convenience, home, ambition, even legitimate enjoyments, to do their duty to souls who needed life. If the man with the Spirit of life is living out his true being, if he is close to the world of sights and sounds, and if he feels the world of joy and grief, how does he hear the call and where does he get the power to do what seems contrary to his basic longings, his very nature? It is simply preposterous to reply that men are restored to life by someone screaming at them to do their duty. It is not that most high ideas don't sound just great; but who wants to carry them out? Ogden Nash sums it up very well:

O Duty,
Why hast thou not the visage of a sweetie or a cutie?
Why glitter thy spectacles so ominously?
Why art thou clad so abominously?
Why art thou so different from Venus
And why do thou and I have so few interests mutually in
 common between us?
Why art thou fifty per cent martyr
And fifty-one per cent tartar?

Why is it thy unfortunate wont
To try to attract people by calling on them either to
 leave undone the deeds they like, or to do the deeds they
 don't?
Why art thou so like an April post-mortem
Or something that died in the ortumn?
Above all, why dost thou continue to hound me?
Why art thou always albatrossly hanging around me?

Thou so ubiquitous,
And I so iniquitous.
I seem to be the one person in the world thou art
 perpetually preaching at who or to who;
Whatever looks like fun, there art thou standing between me
 and it, calling yoo-hoo.
O Duty, Duty!
How noble a man should I be hadst thou the visage of a
 sweetie or a cutie!
But as it is thou art so much forbiddinger than a Wodehouse
 hero's forbiddingest aunt
That in the words of the poet, When Duty whispers low, Thou
 must, this erstwhile youth replies, I just can't.

Duty looks like the "forbiddingest" thing, a military command, extraneous to our nature and foreign to our routine. Life is already dutiful enough for most of us, considering the groceries that must be bought, the rent that must be paid, the boss that must be catered to, the institution that must be obeyed, the rules of the club which must be followed. "Duty" is no more than the code of the microcosm, and all those who manage to end in hell are somewhat surprised, since the boulevard was marked "your duty."

From time to time ministers must work with boys who have been arrested and detained by the authorities. Sometimes the probation officer requests their assistance in a program of counseling. We have found that in cases where the boy has tendencies of the sociopath, he is rarely bothered with pangs of conscience. His highest duty was to receive acceptance from the arrogant little microcosm of his group in exchange for obedience to its every wish. When the leader suggests breaking and entering a home, the members do it, as good soldiers doing their duty.

When Eichmann was on trial in Israel, *Life* magazine editorialized that he was a most unextraordinary fellow. This mass-executioner had no real purpose in living. He looked inside himself and saw a hollow shell. Later, he sold the shell to Hitler, and his fetish-self bore a bright red swastika. Men were forced to parade up and down saluting it—and by "it" is meant both the swastika and (in Eichmann's mind) the fetish. It is interesting how the spirit of evil prostitutes man's great need—to find himself by losing this fetish-self. In Eichmann we see the satanic paradox of the extremely selfish man standing at attention in the most "selfless" response to his duty.

Said *Life*: "Above all he was anxious to please. The obvious Nazi objectives never deterred him, nor did the fact that his best school friend was a Jew. He became a dutiful father and provider and his gross official cruelties never seemed to interfere with his humdrum middle-class German home life. Apart from an aggressive 'German patriotism,' his personality had no sharp edges and his psyche no obvious traumas. What he did with himself could have been done by anyone with an equal talent for keeping his place, 'doing his duty,' taking his orders, and turning his conscience over to the care of the state."

When the *Life* editorial goes on to ask if it was Goethe who said that if you do your daily duty all else becomes clear, it answers that this is obviously false. Behavior must be checked, it concludes, with what we know of right and wrong.

When duty buttresses pride, it becomes "right" in itself and provides its own conscience. Most of what passes for "public morality" is simply respect for a myriad of social cults. The chameleon gods circulate in crowds these days, and as surely as something is fundamentally wrong for the right reasons, it can suddenly become "right" for the wrong reasons. Public officials are hurt when their dishonesty is uncovered—"Doesn't everyone do it?"

As long as the individual continues divorced from himself, an adopted religion of duties may only conceal his true condition. The writers of the New Testament rejected "salvation by good works" as the worst kind of illusion. They considered that man's first task was to get out of his idolizing cult, his false world, immediately, if not sooner. The only way to do this is to unite our spirits with the Spirit of life in Christ and to rejoin the real world which the only God has created in holiness. A man's highest goal is to bring his true being into focus and so be *God's true man*, and his chief duty is to love the Lord his God with his whole being.

Once we are bringing our destiny to fruition, we can envisage our chief duty to our fellows, which is to do what they will permit us to in assisting them fulfill their own destinies. Emerson said, "Our chief want in life is somebody who shall make us do what we can." As my awareness of God in my life grows and I come into fuller possession of myself, I become keenly alive to the pain and triumphs, struggles and joys, of those in the real world. Joined to the Spirit of life, I, too, hunger for the spirits of men. There is only one God, and in Him we are magnetized toward those He has created and is recreating. Only the fullness of life in others can complete my joy in being alive. And now I must go humbly to their back door and beg forgiveness. Too long I have thrown my little world over them, as a painter casts a tarpaulin over a pretty piece of furniture. Their good or evil was in reference to me—now it must be in reference to our one God. If they are convinced that I see and hear them, long to know them both as they are and can be, then they may—I say *may*—listen when I declare the good news—that now their highest duty is not to my old world, but to God's world ever being born, ever new, ever infinitely vast.

I cannot speak for others, but for myself this attitude is extremely difficult to maintain. Let's be honest with each other; how hard it is to be for others. So many times we cannot trust ourselves, even when we profess to be doing someone some good. But we know this—to do our duty we must be able to trust ourselves more every day. Choices must be open to us; we must be able to weigh alternatives with the freedom God affords. Then, on the best knowledge we have, we can love one another as Christ commanded us. If our choices prove to be selfish, we shall be the first to know. The God of freedom will forgive us if we repent. If our love has a convincing measure of sincerity, perhaps the one by whom we were doing our duty shall also forgive us. But this is our confidence: if he does not, because of the resurrection power of the Spirit of holiness, the Spirit of life in Christ, we can still be God's, still be ourselves.

The thesis that only the man in possession of his own soul is morally responsible in the doing of duty is quite simple to validate. Recently I had to spend half an hour in a waiting room. The receptionist, an attractive young lady, was extremely conscious of her own presence, and especially her form-fitting clothes. In one sense she was perfectly oblivious of any other human being on earth, and yet she was talkative with people. For every young fellow who approached the desk she had a disintegrating smile and a spectacular "Hello, there!" Pretty young staff workers were scented with lavish compliments about their clothes; I got the feeling that by complimenting them, she was actually complimenting her own taste; by noticing their attire, she was calling attention to her own. Her job was not getting too much attention, but she was doing her duty as she saw it.

Contrast this woman with Helen Keller, who has a world-famed sense of duty. She should be oblivious to others, because she can't see or hear, and could not since birth. And yet who is more sensitive to their spirits?

Fundamental to our knowledge of life is Jesus' statement of our chief duty. To the question, "Which commandment is the first of all?" Jesus responded by first eliminating the presence of fetishes: "Jesus answered, 'The first is, "Hear, O Israel: The Lord our God, the Lord is one; and you shall love the Lord your God with all your heart, and with all your soul, and with all your mind, and with all your strength." The second is this, "You shall love your neighbor as yourself." There is no other commandment greater than these' " (MARK 12:28–31).

What greater expression of both our love and freedom is there than the duty of encouraging our neighbor to know his own love and gain his own freedom? In countless churches throughout our nation we hear dry ruminations on abstract morality. It seems clear, however, that before we profess to know our duty and the world's as well, we ought to first equip the world through the Holy Spirit with duty-knowing and decision-making powers. It is better to trust a man to do his duty than to constantly tell him what it is. The most that we can do to help him is to acquaint him with the Spirit of life in Christ.

Martin Niemöller once opened his heart with an intimate revelation. He said that God gave him a vision in a dream to make him aware of his personal responsibility for witnessing to others. During the seventh year of an eight-year prison term for defying Hitler, he was startled by the reality of the vision. Previously he had felt no obligation to witness to his Nazi guards of their need for the salvation of Christ. In his dream Hitler was pleading his case before the judgment throne of God. Hitler excused himself on the grounds of never having heard the Gospel. Dr. Niemöller then heard God: "Were you with him a whole hour without telling him of the Gospel?" When he awoke, he remembered that he had indeed been alone with Hitler for a whole hour without witnessing to him of Christ. Immediately he saw that it was his duty to witness to all men, even his guards. The good doctor was so true to his duty that the guards were changed more often lest the Gospel find its mark.

Love for people grows in proportion to our gratitude to God; and gratitude flourishes the more we witness and provide opportunities for His Spirit to reveal the worth and thrilling vitality of life. In gratitude, duty sees its chance in crowds.

One day I parked my car on a main thoroughfare to help a man who was lying in the street after an accident. I did not know if I could do anything for him, but I felt it my duty to be with him, and, if he wished, offer a prayer. Most of the passing motorists were primarily annoyed by the inconvenience. Millions of Americans feel that their highest duty is never to be involved in the troubles of someone else.

In a world of duties left undone, the Christian must think of "love"—a wonderful word that is getting rather obscene in America these days—as one's duty.

A friend told me of an elderly relative of his wife. Her congregation in West Virginia had dwindled down to a handful; then only she was left, and for several months she was the only person in the sanctuary on Sunday mornings—no organist, no minister—only she. That was her place, she felt; finally others heard of her, and the congregation began to grow again.

I went with a church officer to Denver to attend the assembly of our denomination. During that time the elder had to stay in the hospital there for an appendectomy and peritonitis. I stayed with him for two weeks, and there was nothing to do but sit in the hospital room and conduct bedside services morning and evening. One day he pointed to the glass for a drink and said with mock sternness, "Do your duty." We both smiled, and I poured him a drink.

Going back to the hotel, I thought to myself, "Yes, it was my duty, and I wanted to do it. Was it not love's privilege to do the small courtesy?"

When the disciple of the parable gave a cup of cold water, it was not because he recognized Christ, but because he saw his duty. No doubt only Christ will be able to reveal how many good intentions get lost in romantic wishful thinking, while "duty" in overalls passes as "love" in disguise.

If love is filled with emotion, very well; if not, then it must enlist duty as an unfailing ally and do what must be done. Life is at our fingertips if we know what we have to do before we demand others do their duty. Courage these days needs persons with an old-fashioned loyalty to rectitude and a deep devotion to integrity.

In this day when everyone sings about love, and duty is banished to fetish worship, great social issues are being decided. The Christian goes into the streets armed only with God's faith and clear vision. If faith, hope, and joy all falter in the heat of battle, then let God call duty to the colors and win the day. Faith will still be faithful if it knows that somewhere someone is doing his duty.

After a series of spinal operations, Isak Dinesen was in such pain that she had to lie on the floor to dictate to her secretary. Approaching seventy, she knew she must finish her book by working beyond human endurance. She would say to friends that the book probably could not be completed, but then she would finish a page or two more. In time, however, not only was the book finished, but she published two more volumes before her death.

She once said that this experience taught her something important: "When you have a great and difficult task, something perhaps almost impossible, if you only work a little at a time, every day a little, *without* faith and without hope, suddenly the work will finish itself."

Even if one must do an unpleasant task, such as telling an employee that he is fired, one can stand with the one who is hurt in a redemptive way. For duty is not unpleasant—it is the stability of all that is right and good in the world asserting itself at last. It is truth coming in off the scaffold, and it is patience going forth to act. The poet addresses "duty":

> Stern Lawgiver! yet thou dost wear
> The Godhead's most benignant grace;
> Nor know we anything so fair
> As is the smile upon thy face:

Flowers laugh before thee on their beds
And fragrance in thy footing treads;
Thou dost preserve the stars from wrong;
And the most ancient heavens, through thee,
Are fresh and strong.

—William Wordsworth

There is one great strength in learning to trust one's soul. As the years melt away, the "sunset hour" will find us vital in courage and not languishing in indecision.

An elderly minister and his wife began attending services at our church. I learned that emotional problems had caused him to leave the pastorate and take a position in our courts. Several times he preached for us, and though we wondered why he never returned to the pastorate, we never inquired.

One day he called and said that he needed to talk to a minister. I felt ill at ease being a pastor to a minister twenty years my senior. I went to his home.

He told me that he had been called to a small church in another state. The pulpit was open to him once more, and the reality of it troubled him. Before him lay this field of need plus the almost unlimited demands on his time and heart. He said that he did not think he could accept the call. We were conscious that this would probably be his last chance to return to the ministry.

He gave one reason for going, then countered with two for staying. I wasn't sure what to do, so I silently prayed that the Lord would reveal this minister to himself so that he could honestly discuss what was going on inside of him. The more he talked, the more he glued himself to the fence. I looked into his eyes; they were clear and shining—They were trying to see into the future.

Finally, I decided to speak my mind on the matter. I said, "You are an old soldier who cannot believe there is still a place for him in the battle. No doubt the Lord is taking quite a chance. The temptation would hound you to prove yourself by placing the whole kingdom on your own shoulders. You might be long on busy work and short on faith." We were silent for a minute.

"But, on the other hand," I continued, "I am convinced you will go. And why? Because you smell the acrid smoke from the front lines. The struggle with evil for the souls of men is hot in your blood. The call to the wounded sounds in your ears still. To stand up and preach is your meat and drink. You hear the sound of the bugle, and you know full well the Captain is calling you to the colors once more. Oh, you will go, and for one reason—because you know in your heart it is your duty."

Upon hearing that word, he straightened up and brought his shoulders back. He simply said, "Would you lead in prayer, please." Today he is serving that church as its pastor.

Before every lengthening shadow there is the comfort that someone nearby is sufficiently free to be responsive to God's call. That is the stability of human goodness; someone pauses to see the required thing, and does it. God sends these persons to us. What have we that we did not receive, and what could we do did He not nerve us in the very command? "So you also, when you have done all that is commanded you, say, 'We are unworthy servants; we have only done what was our duty' " (LUKE 17:10).

11

Conquer by Backing Off

PEOPLE WHO WALK into our home wonder if we would prefer to live in the jungle. Plants from every corner of the globe are in all our rooms. I am afraid to count them. They are there not only for their beauty, but also because they teach an important lesson.

Each plant has an unwritten pact with God—it will grow only under its own innate conditions. Each plant is like the real self, the genuine *me* of each individual. Given a few basic requirements, each will develop into the integrity of its destined completeness, whether it be the magnificent orchid, with eternal spring breathed into its April petals, or the elegant little *pilea involucrata*, with blooms so small they can hardly be seen.

The secret is knowing when to back off—you can provide the right soil, light, moisture, and humidity, but after that the process is out of your hands. The people whose plants are always dying pressure their plants with too much light, water, and nourishment. They cannot see that growth is from within, and not dependent on pressure from without.

Our lives are infinitely more complex than plants, but our growth is a process that continues in both joy and crises. All necessary effort is expended in fortifying the self to meet each stage of growth. Work is required, and sacrifice, planning, imagination, and faith. But the secret of the life that blossoms is knowing when to back off.

The "American ideal" can degenerate into the notion: "Apply pressure until something gives." A recent poll indicated that the most successful business executives work from morning until night. Too often, however, both executives and employees, students, and housewives become anxiously wrapped up in some goal until they are shaking it furiously —it possesses them.

Blacking out all other thoughts but the crisis at hand results in the pagan dance of "fear." The mind becomes grooved, and the more we think about it, the deeper the circular groove becomes. The wild circular dances of primitive tribes is an impassioned commitment of mind and body to one blind goal.

This is the blind point when all crises take their greatest toll of health and happiness. The creative interaction between our body-minds and the Holy Spirit is short-circuited. Ensuing panic is a feeling of being boxed in and shoved hopelessly to the end of a breaking limb.

Dr. O. F. Rosenow, a teaching physician at Ohio State University's School of Medicine, recently told the Ohio Academy of General Practice that the most common complaint encountered in the practice of medicine is "Doctor, I'm tired." "But the majority of these patients are suffering from a benign type of nervousness; an inability to relax when the opportunity presents itself. They are generally more wound up than run down. Meditation rather than medication is the proper prescription." Dr. Rosenow concluded: "If people learned to shut out the demands of civilization and utilized an hour a day for peace and solitude they wouldn't come so often to physicians' offices."

The ability to apply one's self over a prolonged period is often a valuable asset. But W. G. Carleton once said, "We lay too much stress on stick-to-it-iveness. I once had a professor who wisely hung this sign over his desk: 'Oh, Lord, teach me when to let go.' "

This retreat is not "running away." It is the "foxhole in my mind" President Harry Truman spoke of when referring to his momentary escapes into protective peace and renewal.

It is the "pardon me for a moment" of the labor mediator who excuses himself in the heat of debate to go into another room and look out the window.

It is the "safe place" of I. A. R. Wylie, who wrote: "Sometimes, when things have gone badly, I've found myself running in circles, like a hunted hare with the hounds and hunters at my heels. Then, almost at my last gasp, I have remembered that other self within me who is neither defenseless nor afraid. The frightened, hunted me has taken refuge in that hidden 'safe place' and slammed the gates in the teeth of pursuit."

This is the aloneness with God that the Psalmist had in mind when he declared, "Be still, and know that I am God" (PSALM 46:10).

This sudden withdrawal is a high point of hope. Hopelessness cannot see beyond the next second and demands some glimmer of light *now*. To throttle ourselves until something drastic is done is nothing more than a panicky drive to shake the Artist's hand for a swift completion of the canvas; it is a ruthless tugging at the blossom before it is ready to emerge; it is a pounding on the gates of happiness with bloody hands crying, "Open, *now*."

"Backing off" is an embrace of pure life—it is a moment of transcendence when we disengage ourselves from midstream and stand on the bank with God to survey the whole scene, from the brightness of the waters to the brilliance of the sun. One minister said that in the midst of a sermon when he is "pushing too hard" to make his message effective, he can suddenly withdraw for a split second to see the whole sanctuary, the people with their needs, and the Spirit of God at work.

Just recently we returned from a hectic vacation. We ignored Thoreau's statement, "The swiftest traveler is he that goes afoot," and we shot through ten states and two weeks at breakneck speed. When we got home, we unpacked, exhausted. The next evening we dropped everything, and my wife and I strolled around the block several times as if we were two teen-agers with nowhere to go and nothing to do. We leaned against lampposts, studied the people, chatted on the street corner, and hoped that no passing parishioners would ask if we were lost. It was so enjoyable and refreshing, I was sorry we didn't do this on our vacation. I thought of several leisurely people I knew. So often those who seem to waste time are making the most of it.

A logical conclusion to the problem of mobilizing our energies in stress is this: the more urgently we need answers and the more stressful the situation, the more important it is to back off and gain renewal. Astronaut Alan B. Shepard, Jr., recalls that as the day of the launch approached, he began to feel the effects of tension growing everywhere around him. He found it difficult to pace himself. He said that the first step in effectively meeting this tension is to recognize its presence. Then the attention must be shifted to something else. "The thought of the consequences of an unsuccessful flight were getting to me too much," he said. "So I'd just have to back off and regroup and hit it again."

Concentrate on that which seems to have direct relation to the problem. Rushing to the Bible to find a concrete answer often causes us to feel disappointed—we tend to read our own unconscious feelings into the Word. A more profitable procedure is to objectively list (by writing if necessary) all the factors which pertain to the problem; next list the possibilities; then reckon the resources at hand. If the problem is of a deeply emotional nature, talk to a counselor or minister. A young physicist said that he often talks over his projects with his wife. He relates, "I describe in detail what I'm doing, and she doesn't understand a word. But sometimes, when I'm through, *I* do."

Drop the problem like a hot potato. Concentrate deeply on other verses, some aspect of the kingdom, the nature of God, or what you would like to be doing most. Picture yourself resting confidently in the hand of God.

Early in my ministry I had to adopt a tried and true procedure when backing off. I was being examined by a physician and suddenly found myself quite anxious—the heart was pounding. I feared the worst. Realizing what was happening, I turned my thoughts completely away from the room, pictured a pastoral scene, and *slowly* recited the twenty-third Psalm to myself. After the examination the doctor smiled. When I questioned him, he said that my heart was pounding furiously, but for some reason he couldn't figure out, it went back down to normal in the middle of the examination. When I explained what I had done, he said that his father was a minister and he could understand the stress of this work. Such a use of Scripture that I had employed he thought to be a sound technique.

Many Christians confess that they cannot truly back off

from their problem until they enter the church. The sanctuary helps them transcend cares temporarily while their thoughts are bathed in the presence of God.

A French priest relates that he noticed a young man hurrying into the sanctuary every lunch hour. He would kneel only for a moment, then dart out. The priest edged closer and heard him say simply, "Jesus, it's Jimmy." That was all he ever said. Many years later the priest ministered to this man as he lay dying. On his last visit the priest stopped outside the door and told a friend he had a marvelous experience. He said that he distinctly heard a voice saying, "Jimmy, it's Jesus."

There is great value in the systematic preaching of the Bible. As we hear familiar verses and look around at familiar symbols of grace, our minds take flight back to rich experiences of heaven's goodness. It pays to have a rich bank account of spiritual experiences we can draw upon.

In times of trouble there are many Christians who turn first to the Book of Philippians. There Paul, in prison, had backed off from the world and was joyfully surveying God's work through him. He writes, "Have no anxiety about anything, but in everything by prayer and supplication with thanksgiving let your requests be made known to God" (PHILIPPIANS 4:6).

This was a strange thing for Paul to say, because in II Corinthians 11:28 he recounts terrible hardships and adds, "And, apart from other things, there is the daily pressure upon me of my anxiety for all the churches." Make no mistake, anyone who cares deeply will know anxiety—but anxiety was meant to be a thrust to life, not a style of living.

The first touch of anxiety tells us we have something vital to pray about. When warriors back off for a moment to seek the Lord in prayer, they enter to the throne of grace alone; anxiety cannot enter with them. Prayer is a mountaintop view which brings into focus the widest scope; struggles go on in the valleys, but nothing can keep us from the summit perspective with Christ "where the things of earth grow strangely dim in the light of His glory and grace."

"Sleep" is a backing-off time when the mind is cooled to effectively compute its data. Since sleep is God's will, it serves no useful purpose to box with our problems all night on the mattress. Erasmus once said, "A little before you go to sleep read something that is exquisite and worth remembering, and contemplate upon it till you fall asleep; and when you awake in the morning, call yourself to account for it." Whether your prelude to rest is prayer or good reading, see that the last word of the day is not the whine of anxiety, but a benediction from above.

When the deeps of the soul are ready to bring up an answer from God, it may take a form we never expected. It often comes suddenly, when we are ready to throw in the towel.

Gustave Flaubert tells us this: "The most glorious moments in life are not the so-called days of success, but rather those days when out of dejection and despair you feel rise in you a challenge to life, and the promise of future accomplishments." That promise is probably the most important immediate result of backing off from some pressing problem.

One day a man named Hal walked into my office and asked if I recognized him. I did not. He reminded me that a year previously I had visited his home with an elder from the church, but we left after failing to pry him loose from a wild party. I asked what brought him to see me.

Fortune was not smiling. He was convicted of driving while drunk and was going to lose his job, home, and family. We both agreed his situation could reasonably be called "the bottom." Did I know anyone who could help him? I replied that I did.

"You mean you have connections?" he asked.

"The highest," I replied.

When he pulled his chair closer to the desk, I proceeded to tell him about Jesus, spoken of in John 3 in connection with a nighttime conversation. He was telling Nicodemus that his world would change radically if he were spiritually reborn. Hal's face dropped with disappointment.

"What did I expect from a minister?" he chided himself.

"You are like a man going down in the quicksand of his own emotions," I told him. "You cannot begin to analyze your situation and gain control until a hand from above you reaches down and pulls you out. Only your pride keeps you from raising your hand to meet His."

Hal is a truck driver, and on his last run to Cleveland he

stopped over at a hotel. Like Nicodemus, he could not sleep, and so got up and turned to the New Testament. Fortunately, Christ stays at hotels as well as churches, and Hal met God.

Several months later, after serving several days in jail, he participated in the service of Layman's Sunday, and he told the congregation what happened to him. His wife, family, and friends occupied the first five pews. A profound silence settled over the sanctuary when he finished his story.

He became a mighty influence for good wherever he went, and through him more than one truck driver heard the Gospel in words of one syllable.

One day I made my way to his home to tell him and his wife that their first daughter had just died in childbirth. He slumped over on the edge of the bed as if struck by a terrible blow. The first word to come is always the same: "Why?"

The men in the Sunday morning Fellowship of the Upper Room—some of whom were brought to Christ by Hal—were concerned lest he rebel against all that was sacred. What a victory for evil to have this soldier desert the ranks!

The night before the memorial service, all the men were gathered in the funeral home. The atmosphere prevailing was bleak, but the matter was in God's hands. One of the men felt the need for prayer, and got permission to use an adjoining private room; the other men joined him. They sat quietly for a minute, and then, without a word from anyone, knelt to use the chairs as altars. They took turns praying aloud. When it came Hal's turn, one could feel the fierce storm lashing his soul. There were no pat phrases, only an outpouring of the need to believe that love is crowned by faith beyond the shadows of the grave. When the last "amen" was whispered, one could feel the deep silence that falls like a blanket to cover the trembling earth after a storm. It was a moment of supreme victory over death wrought by the risen Christ, and every man there sensed it fully.

For several years Hal and his wife cared for their granddaughter until her father remarried. Today Hal is an elder who has not gotten over the miracle touch of prayer. Any place at home or on the road is a good place to pray, he feels, and he considers prayer the weight of his particular ministry.

Flesh and blood alone cannot inherit the Kingdom of God.

There is a liberty from the confining world. It is in those moments of transcendence when faith seeks its secret resources that the peace of God brings composure to mind and strength to heart.

12

Your Own Reasons for Living

YOU ARE KNOWN to the world through your work; your religion is known through the way you do it, and your personality through the reasons you do it. All your faculties are channeled into work. Over a lifetime, work is the revelation of what a man is and, therefore, what he wants from life.

Man is reborn so that his true spirit may express itself in labor which fulfills God's purpose. Whatever one professes in church, God will ". . . render to every man according to his works" (ROMANS 2:6,7). All we have said here about duty, gratitude, individualtiy, and spiritual rebirth come into focus in our vocation. Any person can look back over his life and see that his work was chiseled over the proportions of his own soul.

Leo Tolstoy said, "The happiness of man consists in life, and life in labor." This being so, one is appalled by the large number of persons who dislike what they do: employees go through the "motions" for eight hours, hoping the unions will reduce the work time to four hours and then one hour per day, then hopefully to several hours per week; wives hate every minute of housekeeping; there are ministers who despise many of their tasks; laymen who'd like to desert their machines and operate church "machinery" instead, and students who are insulted if you suggest they settle on one occupation—just one.

What would they like to do? What would *you* like to do?

The usual response, "Lounge in a hammock with a friendly glass of lemonade," may mean, "I can tell what I'd like *not* to be doing, but hanged if I know what I could throw myself into."

The great fact of spiritual rebirth is that it gives us the faith to trust God and our own spirit. Possession of one's own spirit is the fabric of self-confidence. And, as Samuel Johnson once commented, "Self-confidence is the first requisite to great undertakings."

The man becoming whole will realistically be convinced of what his spirit prompts him to do, and therefore will do creatively and scrupulously. Commented Lord Rootes, "Starting out to make money is the greatest mistake in life. Do what you have a flair for doing, and if you are good enough at it the money will come." To do this, one must be on good terms with himself. "Happiness" requires knowing God's forgiveness so that one can look into the reality of his own heart, trusting its promptings, feeding its aspirations, training its impulses, and giving voice to its prayers.

Here is the essence of individuality—the important consideration is not that you do what everyone demands, but what your heart requires. Remembering this will enable you to authenticate yourself.

A brilliant young research engineer was recently made manager of his division. He loves problems. He has the courage to put everything aside and stick with a problem, whether or not it promises to unearth any practical know-how. He said that some of the men under him cannot accept problems because of their insecurity—they are so intimidated by failure, that before they proceed very far, they are blaming others for "not assisting in the teamwork." Too often the product of the corporation's training is the well-oiled cog whose self-evaluation is computed by machines and scored by salary increases.

I listened to a group of businessmen at a hunting lodge recently. It was a rousing discussion in which no one listened to the previous speaker, and that's not easy. One man was happy about his manipulation of common stock; another won his place under the sun by selling half a million dollars worth of business a year; another documented his boast that he never buys at retail; another abides religiously by the "rule of gold"

—that it's wise to swindle the competition before they do it unto you.

Sitting back with a grin on his face was the guide and owner of the lodge. Overtly he cared little for money, but he was undisputed king in his domain. On the morrow the party of slick business tycoons would become the fiasco of blundering bufoons, while the guide became the towering sovereign of the little band.

Spending one's self by proving something to the world in behalf of the self is a suffocating job which never seems worthy of the whole person. "Living" becomes the diligent campaign to refute the voices which whisper, "You're worthless." After the hunting guide has proven his point in the winter, I often wonder whether the flowers bloom for him in the springtime, and what life holds for him in summer.

Young persons often ask, "How can I know my calling?"

My answer is, "Look! Be attentive! Become immersed in ideas, in people, in events. Open the mind to every point on the horizon you possibly can. Read the Bible daily. Think a few minutes every day about a great idea. Pray for a sense of responsibility. When you begin to focus on goals and are defeated, ask God whether the goal or profession is reasonably within your grasp. If so, take full responsibility for yourself and your defeat. No excuse was ever good enough. If the goal is beyond you, take yourself in hand, be reasonable, and start from another angle. And whenever you find yourself doing what you do not want to because you are afraid of defeat, write your goals out on a piece of paper. Stare at them. Think about them. Defeats are our most competent teachers, provided we are willing to listen to their instruction. Remember, if there is an insistent voice within you calling you to honor, industry, and competence, God put it there."

Miss Florence Nightingale came from a stylish English family with plenty of money. As a young lady, she sensed the stirrings of a great love, and once asked the Prussian ambassador: "What can an individual do towards lifting the load of sufferings from the helpless and miserable?" Seven years later, her purpose was crystal-clear. She said, "Since I was twenty-four there was never any vagueness in my plans or ideas as to what God's work was for me."

In Miss Nightingale's day, it was unthinkable for a woman of good breeding and elegant manners to do the work of a nurse in public hospitals. She asked Dr. Samuel Gridley Howe, American philanthropist, what he thought of women doing this work. His was a classic response: "My dear Miss Florence, it would be unusual, and in England whatever is unusual is thought to be unsuitable; but I say to you 'go forward,' if you have a vocation for that way of life, act up to your inspiration and you will find there is never anything unbecoming or unladylike in doing your duty for the good of others. Choose, go on with it, wherever it may lead you, and God be with you."

To hear our calling, the heart and mind must be God's, open to His communications. "For what person knows a man's thoughts except the spirit of the man which is in him? So also no one comprehends the thoughts of God except the Spirit of God. Now we have received not the spirit of the world, but the Spirit which is from God, that we might understand the gifts bestowed on us by God" (I CORINTHIANS 2:11,12).

"Safety" as the goal means the certain loss of joy in work. The joy beneath the drudgery makes the difference between existing and living. The excitement of work that makes great demands on us, in its small detail and great challenge, is the difference between putting in our hours and living our vocation.

Henry Cabot Lodge, Jr., has this sense of joy as servant of the country. When he was ambassador in Viet Nam, his work was as exciting as his labors in an office in the Capitol. He said, "I've had a life full of great excitement and great responsibility, and it's the combination of those two that makes life worth living, gives it its flavor. You take those things into account, and you understand that I felt that if there were any way in which I could invest what's left of my life in doing something my country needed, then that's what I should do, whatever the price.

"If you can do something that's worthwhile, that contributes, however little, to your country, and if you can have some fun while you're doing it—why, only a fool would choose to play it safe."

For many years, critics of Freud assumed that the opposite

of "suppression" had to be "free and untamed expression of all instincts." If one opposed the suppression of the heart, he was told, "Oh, you must be a Freudian!"

At the same time, the institutional Protestant church, sheltering the great and respectable middle-class, was forcing souls into its artificial mold. "Do good to thy neighbor" was the theme of the organization-man.

The conservative church was horrified at the thought of being one's true self. The idea of loving and trusting one's self was then, as now, not only heresy, but fiendish (except in deodorant commercials: "If you're not you, you're *nobody*!"). How can one reasonably trust God and himself at the same time? "Impossible!" Of course! It is easier to see humility in futility, and meekness in weakness.

Hitler loved a cause, too, and his expansive-vindictive pride was the end of egotism. We have all been burnt by egotism, and crippled by our own fetishness. We are all a bit envious of the man who seems so sure of where he's going. What we fail to take into account is the fact of "providence." When a man is true to the heart God created, the years of experience will soften, teach, mold, and sweeten him. The years only harden pride. "Pride" is the cloak of weakness. "Humility" is God clothing the strong.

What, then, is "greatness," assuming we must answer this if God calls us to be as great as we can be?

It is, first, *the formation of clear purpose*. Said Powell Buxton, "The longer I live, the more deeply I am convinced that that which makes the difference between one man and another—between the weak and powerful, the great and the insignificant—is energy, invincible determination, a purpose once formed and then death or victory."

This "purpose" is a goal, a telling one's self that finally the truth is out and we have said what it is we must bring to the world, and now there is no turning back. The direction is now clear.

"True purpose" is a declaration of faith in one's self and in God. One feels the urge to express one's self, one *must* to be true, one must not suppress the truth in any man; therefore, what one expresses is true, and God will honor it. If we are created by God, it is imperative that we serve Him by fulfilling the purpose of creation. Other men so minded will rejoice at the fulfillment of ourselves.

Michelangelo was rarely free from the tyranny of other men —he struggled against enemies, jealous rivals, patrons, and circumstances; he longed for solitude and simplicity, and instead he was hounded. But when he was commissioned to decorate the ceiling of the Sistine Chapel, his soul dictated the forms of his frescoes. Since then, men of every race, age, and mentality have studied the divine work and whispered, "Yes."

Every man hopes that his work will endure by the weight of its scope, talent, or integrity. Work that carries God's blessing will endure—it will stand the judgments of time and eternity.

The second mark of greatness is *self-discipline*. Finding and being ourselves as Christ's men has never signified haphazard, inefficient existence. If the self-indulgent, grown-up "baby" would learn to trust the calling of vocation, he would have had the ability to submerge distractions and lesser goals into the spiritual industry which brings reality out of dreams.

I think of Miss Nightingale again. In the hospital in Crimea, patients witnessed amputations in the wards. Dead horses lay in the conduit which carried drinking water. Conditions of sanitation were so bad that they could not be described accurately. Dying women of ill-repute entertained dying soldiers in the basement. The "Lady with the Lamp" sailed for Scutari in 1854 with thirty-eight volunteer nurses. In the next three years she discovered that her most formidable obstacles were really pettiness, suspicion, disloyalty, and outright hostility from politicians and army brass. She believed in what she was doing, and her patience seemed inexhaustible.

In 1869 she learned that one of her nurses was losing her temper and becoming a martyr in a one-woman campaign. Miss Nightingale wrote to her. "Do you think I should have succeeded in doing anything if I had kicked and resisted and resented? I have been shut out of hospitals, obliged to stand outside the door in the snow, have been refused rations for as long as 10 days at a time for the nurses I had brought by superior command. And I have been as good friends the day after with the officials who did these things—have resolutely ignored these things *for the sake of the work*."

Shortly before he died, Thomas A. Edison was asked the secret of his success. He answered, "Two things that had nothing to do with my knack of inventing things had a lot to do with it. One was good luck. The other was that nobody was ever able to convince me that it was unfair to my fellow workers to put forth my best efforts in my work. I'm glad there was no such thing as the eight-hour day when I was a young man. I won't say it isn't a boon to others, but if my own life had been restricted to eight-hour days, I don't think I would have accomplished a great deal. This country wouldn't be what it is today if the young men of fifty years ago had been afraid that they might earn more than they were paid for."

Jesus once told a one-sentence story. The parable is in Matthew 13:44: a man discovered a hidden treasure and sold all that he had to buy that field; he did it joyfully; the transaction was his all in exchange for the best—he gladly sacrificed the expendable for the indispensable.

The fact that Florence Nightingale was a woman of enormous energy and capabilities does not excuse persons of lesser ability from greatness. It is not inability, but the lack of dedication, which is sapping the resources of humanity. No one knows what he is capable of doing until he is ready to sacrifice all to do it.

George Bernard Shaw thought about hard work in this light: "I am of the opinion that my life belongs to the whole community, and as long as I live it is my privilege to do for it whatsoever I can. I want to be thoroughly used up when I die, for the harder I work, the more I live. I rejoice in life for its own sake. Life is no 'brief candle' for me. It is a sort of splendid torch which I have got hold of for a moment, and I want to make it burn as brightly as possible before handing it on to future generations."

The third mark of greatness is *the willingness to go it alone*. All of us rejoice in agreement; harmony makes for tranquility. As soon as someone steps out of line, we are alarmed—"What is he trying to do?"

The cost of following one's calling in integrity often means paying a high price in loneliness. It is because the spirit of whole men is in such openness with the spirit of the race that it feels keenly the separation of having to go it alone. The fetish-worshipper feels isolated, but those who love deeply know loneliness. But individuality is able to bear it. "Integrity" is an investment in the future.

Lincoln is no doubt the man who was the individual of his time, and now we identify him as "the man of all men." Tolstoy said he was "a universal individualist." With three exceptions, he was defeated every time he put himself into a political campaign. After each defeat he returned to law practice without animosity or cynicism, but determined to brood, to think, to study issues, and to listen to God. He entertained the call of destiny. The incoming tide of God's moral law was washing upon the granite of his soul, and he stood upon its peaks and fastened his eyes on the horizon to see the dayspring of God's will. Later critics were not agreed in their evaluation of Lincoln's goal: "My paramount object is to save the Union, and not either to save or destroy slavery. . . ." Lincoln pondered to precipitate the basic issue. To him no basic institution of free men could be guaranteed without a free and democratic government to safeguard the rights of all. Therefore, the democracy must be preserved.

A state convention was scheduled in Bloomington, Illinois, to reorganize the Republican Party. There was heated opposition to the spread of slavery to the Nebraska Territory. Orators stabbed the air with shrill cries for action. Suddenly there were calls for Lincoln to speak. He had no hesitancy. The music in his soul was being composed for many years, and he had simply to amplify himself for others to hear the crecendoes of justice. The audience was transfixed. Reporters forgot to record what he said, but some experts today guess that this might have been Lincoln's greatest message.

Once he knew that the depths of him had given birth to the great fact of history, his heart became light itself for the remainder of his career. What is this fact? It is that men were born to freedom, and the Republic exists to guarantee it. Citizens must have a free government to champion the rights of majority and minorities. This separates Lincoln from the superpatiotic generals and politicians for whom the glorious state is a projection of the pride-bound self. Cried Lincoln: "Thanks to all. For the great Republic—" but he did not end there. He added, ". . . for the principle it lives by and keeps alive—for man's vast future—thanks to all."

Only the subsequent destiny of America could provide the final verdict on Lincoln. As far as some contemporaries were concerned, John Hay wrote that it was "absurd to call him a modest man."

The fourth gauge of greatness has little to do with "energy" or "solitude"—it must be *the cause to which one is dedicated.* This is the avenue that is quite accessible to eternal life. Said Phillips Brooks, "The ideal life is in our blood and never will be still. Sad will be the day for any man when he becomes contented with the thoughts he is thinking and the deeds he is doing,—where there is not forever beating at the doors of his soul some great desire to do something larger, which he knows that he was meant and made to do."

See, now, the supreme importance of *Christian* vocation. The dedication of what we do to the glory of God places us in the rank of Christian ministers. Occasionally a man must abandon his pursuits to engage in work that is in line with his calling. Jesus did not want to call Peter when he was a failure, so He filled Peter's boat with fish. It suddenly dawned on Peter that the complete giving of himself to fish, with Christ in his situation, was a mockery of His God-enabled prospects. Christ had no argument with Peter's need to fish; He said, in effect, "Peter, I do not call you because you are a failure as a fisherman, but as a success. In fact, you are too successful just for fish. You ought to be throwing out your net for men."

Whether one changes occupations or not, one ought to keep fervently alive his Spirit-fed appetite for ventures among people that transcend the tiny fortunes of the day. Many in this life are not going to be making money at what they would love most to do. It dawns slowly on some of us that our brightest dreams are going to glitter in mothballs; our eyes stop straining to see the most distant castles, and we call it more our "common sense" than so many painful disappointments which cause us to enjoy the distractions and to languish longer at the rest stops. There will have to be richer satisfaction than receiving the gold watch after thirty years' service. It will have to be something to be felt and lived day by day.

Said Dorothy L. Sayers: "I ask that work should be looked upon, not as a necessary drudgery to be undergone for the purpose of making money, but as a way of life in which the nature of man should find its proper exercise and delight and so fulfill itself to the glory of God."

In 1957 three alcoholics in the process of being cured had four dollars. They convinced a Manhattan landlord to lease them a vacant nightclub—Fellowship Center in New York City is the fulfillment of that vision. Not only men who are alcoholics, but also their wives and children, receive counsel, food, lodging, and hope there.

Retirement may be the time when you can devote increased energy to a work that holds a special place in your heart. James F. Byrnes devoted his life to politics. Director of War Mobilization, he also served from 1945 to 1947 as secretary of state under President Truman. After thirty years in federal service, beginning as a U.S. Senator, he came home to South Carolina and served as Governor from 1950 to 1954. Almost all his time nowadays is devoted to the James F. Byrnes Foundation, which provides scholarships to orphans. The foundation began its work in 1948, and he has turned over to it returns and royalties from all of his speeches and articles, plus money from the sale of his beach house at the Isle of Palms near Charleston. Grants have been the means of giving a college education to 265 young people.

This kind of inspiration forces us into creative work that usually involves as much routine work and a mountain of details as any job. But we force ourselves into *every* aspect, carried on by the tremendous worth of the whole career and disciplined to go beyond our best. Here is the Christian faith tested by works. A framework of faith and doctrine hovers over us "out there" as the way we'd like the world to be, and to which we retreat in moments of religious emotion.

Someone says, "What is the Christian point of view on that?" or "Let us have a word of prayer," and off we go into this celestial orbit, with appropriate thoughts and gestures. But the closing of the gap between heaven and earth is the call of the most famous prayer, and only by the earthy feel of a drop of sweat, other hands, and the yoke of solid events are we able to know the length and breadth of God's power.

Today we are being thrust with lightening rapidity into a technical and social revolution which will increase productivity by cybernation and decrease man-hours labor. We see already what this has done to the unemployed, whose heart beat in a machine. We see what poverty has done to the millions in America who have yet to know the integrity and self-fulfillment of daily labor with a wage worthy of the laborer. Depersonalization may well strike the rich and poor alike who sit back and watch a gadget run their world. Escapism for some will run rampant. Some will hunt, hoe, tinker, or plug until they die. But others . . .

. . . There will be countless others who see the curse of labor being replaced by the blessing of work through Christian vocation. After all, women who have watched their children make homes of their own have had to face similar problems. Now that the world goes its merry way, should it stop for them to get off and die? At forty-five years of age, with their mature years of strength and wisdom before them?

Betty Friedan, author of *The Feminine Mystique*, calls this day a "massive breakthrough" for American women. Their entrance into new work, exciting businesses, and their education in vast new skills thrusts them to the zenith of "the fourth dimension." She says (first quoting a housewife): "'Actually, it's suddenly feeling that you are part of the world before and the world after, of something bigger than you are. And the excitement of making your own ideas become realities. You can sit around and talk till hell freezes over, but it's just daydreaming unless you have the courage to take the next step, and get personally committed to real action that tunes you in to other people, and to the community.' . . . The emergence of this fourth dimension involves a subtle but profound change in the whole *Gestalt* of women's lives, changing the way they see themselves, and the way others see them; posing new problems for women, men and society; creating new patterns in marriage, motherhood, homemaking, education and all the professions, even impinging on American politics and the national economy."

The church has an open door before it. In this age people will have time . . . time . . . time to reveal their souls. What shall any man be? What shall he stand before the whole world and become? He can turn to any direction and find a million hands stretched out to him. "Come and be with us, come work with us," they all cry. Now the human spirit must bear fruit as never before or be buried in an ignominious avalanche of trivia.

So it has been with the people in the procession of splendor who have echoed Lincoln's words, "Thanks to all." Thanks be to life, with its terrors that shock us into attention and its wonders that charm us into adoration. Thanks be to brothers on a small planet, some of whom love us and many who need us enough to make loneliness a nobility and not a curse. Thanks be to Christ, who knows our broodings and black moods, and promises that the violent conflicts of time are the birth pangs for the will of God. And thanks to God, who has carved out a place for us in this drama spanning the ages, and has called us to it that we might be in the flow of life.

"And whatever you do, in word or deed, do everything in the name of the Lord Jesus, giving thanks to God the Father through him" (COLOSSIANS 3:17).

Oh, thanks be to God for life, and to life for God! In Him our work is joy!

A Prayer

Let me do my work each day;
And if the darkened hours of despair overcome me,
May I not forget the strength that comforted me
Walking over the silent hills of my childhood,
Or dreaming on the margin of the quiet river,
When a light glowed within me,
And I promised me early God to have courage
Amid the tempests of the changing years.
Spare me from bitterness
And from the sharp passions of unguarded moments.
May I not forget that poverty and riches are of the spirit.
Though the world know me not,
May my thoughts and actions be such
As shall keep me friendly with myself.
Lift my eyes from the earth,
And let me not forget the uses of the stars.
Forbid that I should judge others,
Lest I condemn myself.
Let me not follow the clamor of the world,
But walk calmly in my path.

Give me a few friends who will love me for what I am;
And keep ever burning before my vagrant steps
The kindly light of hope.
And though age and infirmity overtake me,
And I come not within sight of the castle of my dreams,
Teach me still to be thankful for life,
And for time's olden memories that are good and sweet;
And may the evening's twilight find me gentle still.

—Max Ehrmann

13

Life Encounters Death

IT IS SAID in the Bible that the last enemy to be destroyed is death. We deal with him at last, because all that we have said about the reality of life are phantom meanings if the light of life cannot shine in the valley of the shadow. For at the end of all our searching paths there stands the omnipotent tyrant. When he calls, all heed; when he beckons, all go.

When we examine the lives of men who loved life in all its reality, we do not find that they spun a web of poetic fantasy over death. Death for them, too, wounded and plundered. The spaces left in their hearts were as vacant as for any whose lonely love may rest but never vanish.

But for these Christ restored the hunger for the life eternal, and satisfied it. Both the urges to live and love and their fulfillment were so insistent that one's sole conclusion was simply that, while creation existed and perished, the sons of God received life as a gift.

It is doubtful that, for as long as men live, they ever completely lose the hunger for a life so boundless it transcends the confines of time and space. "If the treasure is not anywhere," says Celia in T. S. Eliot's play *The Cocktail Party*, "why do I feel guilty at not having found it?" In the forgiveness for sins which separated him from the creating life of God, the pilgrim receives the Spirit of life. This Spirit is his guarantee that the full inheritance of this life is found past the edge of time.

What, then, is this sinister thing which robs persons of the hunger for life, and makes them prey to the fear of death?

The Apostle Paul responds "To set the mind on the flesh is death. . . ." (ROMANS 8:6).

What does he man by "the flesh"? The "flesh" is the term for our concrete human condition, as molded by history, our culture, and our own personal pattern for manipulating the world around to a more comfortable position. The flesh is the arena where sinners wear fetish masks, the ideas-about-us through which we hope to find glory or die of fear.

This flesh with which we are clothed has become the ground of our separation from God. Fetishes compete on the open market: behind them, many are selling, but few are buying; many long to receive, but few give; many talk, but few listen; many are waiting, but few are providing. Many hucksters in the stalls are privately selling themselves. Selfness in fruition is suppressed. Selfishness blatant is everywhere.

Many are glaring at reflections; few are perceiving the world. Many are searching for symbols of glory; few perceive the signs of the times. Many adore in the open; few love in their hearts. Many seek to keep the symbols of the flesh eternal; few accept the eternalness of the Spirit. Death chastises many; few are saved.

The hope of hitching the immortality of the soul to the trappings of the flesh signifies the immobilization of logic. As pastor, I often drive in funeral processions, and I observe the faces of pedestrians we pass. Some look away sharply, pretending not to see; some stare right through us; others turn away in disgust; a few look angry at this rude intrusion.

A life insurance company took over Steinway Hall in New York City. One of the company's first acts was to have workers chisel off the angels which decorated the facade of the building. Life-insurance people want to sell insurance for the future, without anyone thinking of death. Salesmen say, "If something should ever happen to you, your children will be well taken care of." If *what* should ever happen?

As the final touch of macabre elegance, refusal to recognize the implications of the immortality of the soul leads persons to cherish the flesh in death as in life. A firm in the Midwest advertises embalming by refrigeration—the company calls it "The Humane Way." But one memorial park in the East beats them all—this bastion against the skies advertises a mausoleum of granite, steel, and reinforced concrete to combat nature's forces. The ad reads, "The entire structure is hurricane-proof, and is an outstanding example of the latest in mausoleum design and construction. You will find great peace of mind in knowledge that your loved ones rest secure in the lasting protection of ______ Mausoleum."

The prevailing philosophy concerning death is that it is an event that happens in the indefinite future. This attitude conveniently seeks to ignore death as a process which is very much a part of the present life. Death is the fragmentation of living, and the consequences of losing the unity of the Spirit of life.

The separation of ethics from spirited self-realization means the death of personal morality. The separation of sex from the unity of the self means the death of love. Separation of function within the physiological unity of the organism means disease and suffering. The conflicting cleavage of emotions and purposes through idolatry, with its consequent neurosis, is the paralysis of the true self. The separation of both the true self and its "idols" from all reality is "psychosis" (serious mental derangement).

The separation of the true self from God through the deceit of sin is the beginning of death. This is truly tragic, for then there is no way for the self to revive itself. Courage is lost, and there is no power to retrieve hope; joy is lost, and there is no power to believe in happiness; faith falters, and there is no power to trust deeply; self-esteem flounders, and there is no power to be honest; inspiration is lost, and there is no desire to behold beauty; prayer is lost, and there is no desire to serve. People fade, and with them the desire to live fades.

Lost souls fear death, but may frantically long for death as release from the fear of death. Death appears as judgment. A voice seems to whisper, "If life could not unmask this dress rehearsal for eternity, then death will not be so charmed by deceit."

Death is not the cause of our troubles—it is the judgment of God upon them. "The wages of sin is death" (ROMANS 3:23). Death is the verdict upon separation. The glorification of flesh is the death of the soul, and the death of the flesh is the prelude to God's judgment upon the soul. God's pronouncement in eternity is His judgment upon the role-playing of time, and eternal separation from God—the second death—is a consequence of the enmities of the present.

Death is very much a part of life—it is a judgment upon each succeeding moment. Life is through the Spirit of Christ; and Christ judges the self-realization, for Christ is the agent of creation of the full glory of each individual self. What the self may be through the power of the Spirit of God is known only to Christ, the Son of Man. The judgments of eternity are the open and final declarations of those persistent enlightenments Christ has revealed upon thought and deed. "For as the Father has life in himself, so he has granted the Son also to have life in himself, and has given him authority to execute judgment, because he is the Son of man" (JOHN 5:26,27).

Death is judgment rising to inexorable climax. The death of each man around us is the crescendo. The glory of God is inescapable—it shames those who determine to divorce their lives from it. The realization of God's glory through the Spirit is the true preparation for beholding the full glory of God. Before God's judgments in eternity, it will be seen that those who separated themselves from the glory of the Spirit of life in Christ separated themselves also from each other and from God.

The judgments of death are the prelude to life. When men are open to judgment, they sense how death must be overcome by the love which brings separations to an end. Nicholas Berdyaev has said that we would all have Christian attitudes if we saw men as if we all were dying. "A person who is dying calls forth a special kind of feeling. Our attitude to him is at once softened and lifted on to a higher plane. We then can feel compassion for people whom we did not love. But every man is dying, I too am dying and must never forget about death."

On Nov. 22, 1963, death made captive the President of the United States—John F. Kennedy fell, and left a void filled by horror and grief. Americans then grew hostile toward hate—at least for a time. Strangers consoled each other on the street. Aching hearts huddled together on a small planet in a universe of loneliness. In the presence of unbearable cruelty, men sought life and found love.

In Dallas, Texas, several men in public places spoke out

in judgment on community life that is flooded with suspicion. This judgment brought down cries of "Communist!" "Traitor!" on their heads. One prominent executive of an oil firm lost his job because of the adverse publicity resulting from his temerity. Following judgment, there was suffering, then sorrow, then repentance, then fetish-sacrifice, then rebirth. But not all men are redeemed by the sacrifices of a noble few.

Only the sacrifice of Christ can reverse the course of death and enable us to receive the Spirit of life as a gift. Christ partook of our nature ". . . that through death he might destroy him who has the power of death, that is, the devil, and deliver all those who through fear of death were subject to lifelong bondage" (HEBREWS 2:14,15).

The closing chapters of the Book of John carry Christ's uppermost thought to us—the Son of God must die for our sakes! therefore, let us love one another. He died as a prelude to His resurrected life. The crucifixion of our fetishes is the prelude to a resurrected life with Him, beginning here and now, and expressed primarily in love.

The singular sign that any man has received the Spirit of life and is now gloriously involved in self-realization is his restoration to mankind. "We know that we have passed out of death into life, because we love the brethren. He who does not love remains in death" (I JOHN 3:14).

Love speaks of the restoration of life. Where love prevails, the fear of death is conquered. While death reigns, separation continues unabated; then death becomes its own judgment. When life reigns, love comes into its freedom; then life vindicates itself by the very living of it.

With the British, the Rev. Dr. Ernest Gordon was a prisoner of the Japanese, captured during the building of the bridge over the River Kwai in Thailand. Daily the men were tortured, beaten, and starved, and hundreds were butchered. Camp conditions were beyond description. One day he knew he had diphtheria. He was left in the Death House to die slowly. He observed the men of the camp—they had become like animals. Loneliness was everywhere. The air reeked with death. No one knew his neighbor. Pride had no defense except pure, bare, animal pride. Every man hated the rest for being like himself.

There was fighting and stealing for bits of garbage, a scrap of cloth. Filth covered filth. Latrines overflowed. The monsoons were in, and the floor of his hut was a sea of mud. Religion was nonexistent. Death was faced in the narcosis of fuming arrogance. This was the victory of corruption breeding the vermin of despair.

Two men did not submit to this assault on dignity—one was a Roman Catholic and the other a Methodist. Dinty and Dusty offered to clean Gordon and serve him.

Both men loved the individuality of persons, the subtle graces of each flower, the unique place of common things. They were fed on hope.

One day Gordon asked Dusty what he wanted to do when he got out. He replied that he longed to work with young people in a church. Gordon wanted to know if he hoped to do any good.

"Why, when you work with people, there's always good to be given and good to be received. At least I've always found it so; haven't you, sir?"

Day by day, Dusty's hope became more contagious. It was having an effect of aliveness on the beaten soldiers. Gordon could not understand it, and tried to contradict this layman with reason. He insisted that life had no purpose, and Dusty was positive that it did, even in that place of unspeakable filth and suffering. Commented Dusty, "We have to go on living and hoping, having faith that life is stronger than death. Only God can give life. We have to receive it—and that daily."

A miracle of love restored faith and life to the camp. A Bible study group was organized. The men fastened the eyes of the soul upon Jesus. They went to Him just as they were. They approached Him through prayer. He revealed Himself as the Resurrection and the Life. He embraced sinners, and gave them the gift of the eternal Spirit of life. And what was the effect?

The effect was that the men saw Jesus in His crucifixion as suffering with them, and in His resurrection as infusing them with the energy of God's divine nature. The Spirit imparted life to spirit. Men aided each other, pooled their resources, came to know and love each other, cared for wounds, praised God in voice and instrument, served Holy Communion, and constructed a church. Ernest Gordon, the skeptic, found reason helpless in the face of death, but found life in Christ's Spirit by faith. Today this man is dean of the chapel at Princeton University.

"In this is love perfected with us, that we may have confidence for the day of judgment, because as he is so are we in this world. There is no fear in love, but perfect love casts out fear. For fear has to do with punishment, and he who fears is not perfected in love. We love, because he first loved us" (I JOHN 4:17–19).

Said Catherine Marshall: "Every time I have had depth-dimension fellowship with a friend . . . or have seen even a modicum of love let in to transform a sour human relationship, I have had a preview of immortality. Every time I have had real joy, I have glimpsed eternal life."

The Rev. Walter Robert Matthews was Dean of St. Paul's Cathedral in London. He once broadcast a series of talks on immortality which brought nineteen-hundred letters from listeners. The Dean commented: "If there is any lesson to be learned from the letters I have had, it is that love is the main source of the desire for life beyond death."

As time passes, Christ Himself becomes the ever-present vindication of the holy life. To love for His sake is to share in the life of eternity here and now. Those who say, "One world at a time, please," have never made much sense to me. When questioned, they say that they think of earth as one world and heaven as another totally unrelated drama somewhere above the clouds. How childish to think this, and how easy, unless we have access in one Spirit to the Father.

In this life He is forever calling us to the impossible, and being crucified for our failures. All our years we love just enough to catch a glimpse of the glory of God's nature. We plan long enough to see some of our dreams crumble, and we live righteously long enough to know the utter sinfulness of sin. We have had the balm of kindness to heal our separations just long enough to know how much we might have cared—and the years are forever behind us. The more we aspire, the more we know the spires of dearest hope will not be seen by us on this side. The clearer the imprint of the Son of Man becomes on our own lives, the more the flesh denies our powers to be faithful to Him; and so we who claim His life share His crucifixion. This is partially why we are men of two worlds —We have His promise that those who share His crucifixion shall also, by the power of God, share the victory of His resurrection.

"Just as we have borne the image of the man of dust, we shall also bear the image of the man of heaven. I tell you this, brethren: flesh and blood cannot inherit the kingdom of God, nor does the perishable inherit the imperishable" (I CORINTHIANS 15:49,50).

Rarely have I rested the case for eternal life with the descriptions of metaphysical contact between this dimension of life and the next, although I do not doubt the reality of these phenomena. I believe our case must rest with what we personally know of Christ's power to impart life through His eternal Spirit.

A minister wrote to his wife, outlining funeral arrangements for the time when he would die. He had a beautiful service planned, but added, "No sermon, please. Words are awkward at such a time." Not so for myself. We have heard often a simple story of the sacrifice and resurrection of the Son of Man. The oft-repeated whisper never fails us, ". . . because I live, you will live also" (JOHN 14:19). If someone near and dear were to pass on, I would want the preacher to tell the story again. I fear I would lose my sense of propriety and stand up in the middle of the sermon and say, "Pastor, go over that part again, would you please? Where the angel said, 'He is not here. He is risen.' Tell us that once more." Oh, I believe the story now. But if I ever believed it, I would surely believe it then. I hope in that hour we shall not be treated to poetry and honey-dipped phrases. When the chill of the brief void seems unbearable let some man of simple heart and strong faith declare this truth, "For as in Adam all die, so also in Christ shall all be made alive" (I CORINTHIANS 15:22).

The news of the death of someone we know is the ever-swirling eddies of eternity reminding us that we stand only for a moment on an island of time. I, for one, want to hear the Gospel of Christ before that step. "Tell me the story always, if you would really be; In any time of trouble, A comforter to me." It is good to love, for we can remember those whom we comforted on the island's edge. Then, one day, we can say, "Death, servant of God, do you think after I have met you so often you look any different to me now? My Saviour's people found you a defeated foe, and I find you so now. I see before me all the faces of those exalted by joy, conquerors with mortal wounds, and all their courage is bequeathed to me. Old foe, I know you well. Lead me home."

Sometimes I meet persons who look ten or even twenty years older than they are in age. They want to recapture youth. Actually, they want to recapture life. Death presses on their spirits. They ask what to do.

What must you do to have life? First, take a long, hard look at what you really want from the world. What do you expect people to do for you? How do you blackmail them? What do you hide behind?

Then, go to Christ honestly, and ask the Spirit of life to dwell in your entire personality. The Spirit of life is the Spirit of Christ. Jesus said that we should figuratively "feast" on Him. "As the living Father sent me, and I live because of the Father, so he who eats me will live because of me. This is the bread which came down from heaven, not such as the fathers ate and died; he who eats this bread will live for ever" (JOHN 6:57,58).

Having received the witness of the Spirit that God's nature has infused your spirit and that you are spiritually reborn into the realm of God's glory, trust yourself. Come to love your true nature, with all its powers created in the image of God. Cultivate your true being. Fill the mind with Bible thoughts, good books, excellent verse, great ideas. Be filled with ideals, far-off goals, rich dreams.

O God, when our time seems short
and our responsibilities seem long
and our mood is heavy, full of pressure,
grant us a great thought.

O God, when we count the days before us
and the days behind,
but when their effort seems for trifles or for naught,
when our habits and our patterns and relationships
bind our lives with cutting but invisible chains,
grant us a great thought.

Grant us again, O God, a great thought
when sorrow drops upon us,
when situations make us worriers instead of warriors,
when we are weary with programs
and with projects and with people.

And Father, in the circumstances where we stand alone,
judged by ourselves but not enough forgiven,
shaken by the loneliness of never being fully comprehended
or even cared about or listened to,
grant us then, O God, another great
sustaining thought.

O God, whose works are open but whose workings
hidden,
when we look into the context of our world
and our experience,
when we see our possibilities
and our impossibilities,
and are ready, not to rest and rise again,
but to resign,
save us from the silent shriek of our surrender,
uplift us with that hand that out of darkness
flung out light,
and for the sake of those whose lives are structured
in the art or artlessness of ours,
do thou, O God of all our expectations and endurance,
grant us a great thought.

When the mind is filled with great thoughts, it is ready to tackle great problems. Subscribe to a good news magazine and a good daily paper, and keep abreast of events around the world. See the issues. Join forces with righteousness.

Then find your place of service. Give yourself. Be grateful for life, and do your duty for its sake. Love graciously and serve faithfully, so that people may depend upon you. Work through the church, and in the world. Do the hard thing for the sick, the poor, the needy, the downtrodden. And when you do, at all costs resist the forces of death which seek to compromise your integrity. Flee the symbols of pride, self-satisfaction, and pharisaism. When you find yourself dependent on the glory of men, go to your pastor or a professional counselor and open up your anxieties, regrets, and hostilities.

Express gratitude to God for beauty, love, and truth wherever you find it. See faults, but overlook them. See goodness, and aid it. Live hopefully. The true glory of anyone is what he can be through God's patient power. To aid another in loving life is the mark of true greatness, and to live as great as we can be is the duty of all mankind.

Above all, trust God. Do not overload people with your goodness, which is purported to be for their benefit, in order that they become indebted to you. Persons should be free to live their own lives and come to their own decisions. They must be trusted; and when they fail, trust God. He has ways with people we know nothing of; and when we pray for them, it is not the least, but the most, we can do.

Trust God. When you disgrace yourself, and part of you dies prematurely, think of how far He has already brought you, and trust Him. Said an old Negro slave preacher, "We ain't what we ought to be and we ain't what we want to be and we ain't what we're going to be. But thank God, we ain't what we was."

And when He takes His own precious jewel, trust Him then.

There is in heaven a beautiful young lady. Ten years ago I confirmed her. I never new anyone like her, considering her age. She had the perception of an aged saint. When she prayed, I sometimes looked through my fingers to see if she were reading.

This girl wrote psalms—they were gems of simple devotion. She and the Lord walked as one. When she discussed Scripture, I would look up at the painting of the boy Christ in the temple. Her words fell with rare grace and charm, and she had something to teach when she spoke.

I once visited her home and was surprised to find her outside, playing some wild game—this child could be as carefree and foolish as any other youngster of thirteen. In high school, she was into more things than a politician; and when some absurdity tickled the right bone, she'd have everyone laughing at her own hilarity.

If I ever write a text on psychology, I believe I'll devote a chapter to her. Hers was a broken family. Some people considered her father to be irresponsible, that he rarely bothered with his home. They thought her mother to be uneducated and at times rather coarse, but she loved the girl; she attended church only two or three times, once when Patricia was confirmed.

I made plans for this girl. Imagine what she would be at twenty-three! At forty-three! It was quite a responsibility being pastor to this potential leader in the church.

None of this was to be. She stayed one day at her grandmother's, and her dress caught fire when she was cooking the meal—she was burned from head to toe. When she lay in the hospital, the church prayed night and day. Several beds from her was a woman of the streets who had taken poison; some of her organs were locked in the same way as the girl's. They received the same treatment, and were attended by the same doctors; the woman recovered, and the young girl died.

Her funeral service was held in church. I read the words of Jesus, "Little girl, I say to you, arise" (MARK 5:41). Songs of victory were sung.

Christ, who had the power to raise Lazarus, wept at his death and at Patricia's. It was a delicious satisfaction to know that God would one day do what is so simply and glibly expressed, and He would do it to shame the sophisticated—He would raise her from the dead and restore her to the church.

Later her mother came to the office and gave some of her possessions to me. I went to the empty sanctuary, and placed her offering envelopes in the plate. I returned to a pew and opened her New Testament: "March 29, 1953. To Patricia ______; for excellent scholarship and effort in the 1953 confirmation class."

What does her memory leave us with? Thoughts of death? No. The memory of her feeds our urge to live. If God desires to take a costly jewel, He will follow His own counsels. I have ceased measuring life in the scales of time. If God took His own Son at thirty-three, he would not hesitate to take a daughter at thirteen. She accomplished more in a few years than many do in seventy, and we are grateful that He gave the woman in the hospital time to discover her purpose in life.

I had a confirmation class recently, and I decided to give the same New Testament to another promising girl. Why should I keep it any longer? The Word of God is not a token of memory, but the news of new life. Let the Book make other such girls, and thus be a tribute to its first owner. The most fitting response to a good life is for us to live. When those you love leave, do you not feel a greater responsibility to carry their light, a more pronounced upsurge of their life leading you ahead? This is God's plan.

Blessed are those who, in their death, call us to live! There is only one life and one Spirit. If death cannot separate us from Him, then we may grieve in the night, but we shall laugh in the sun. For God wills that we live forever.

"To the King of ages, immortal, invisible, the only God, be honor and glory for ever and ever. Amen" (I TIMOTHY 1:17).

14

The Breath of God

INTO WHATEVER OR whomever God breathes, life arises. In Hebrew, the word for "breath," "spirit," and "wind" is the same. In Greek, the word for "spirit" and "wind" is the same. In Genesis, chapter 1, it is written that the "breath of God" moved over the face of the waters. In Genesis 2:7, it is said that God breathed into man's nostrils the breath of life and he became a living being. All things are bound to the Creator by the moral and physical laws, known and unknown, and are sustained in structure and attributes by the Word of His power.

The breath of God is in man, and his spirit is immortal. The marks of God are indelibly on that spirit. The stirrings of truth, goodness, and love for unity are suffocated by sin, but they are as basic to man's nature as his need to breathe. Man was created to be at home with the divine nature. The divine breath is invisible. The worship of visible fetishes drives the life from us and alienates us from our own nature, but the homing instinct is never completely lost.

Whatever their creed, men know that when goodness, love, and truth stir within them, God is still living. Jesus said that when the Son of Man returns in His glory, He will sit on His throne. The nations will be gathered for judgment. The blessed righteous gave Him care and compassion, although they did not know they were serving Him: "Truly, I say to you, as you did it to one of the least of these my brethren, you did it to me" (MATTHEW 25:40).

When men are at home with themselves, they are at home in the fellowship of brothers. The one birthmark is not in our flesh, but in our spirit. To be at home with God, one must be equally at home with the spirit of man. Whoever is too anxious about the worth, depth, and capacity of the human spirit as both the handiwork and field of God, is too handicapped to be fully used as an instrument of God in the world. The tip-off that any one man is a stranger to himself is that he builds high walls against others before he knows them. Eventually he builds walls automatically on all sides, assuming that all neighbors feel as he does. The evidences of God in the general revelation are not decoded, because he cannot permit himself to entertain any compulsion to tear down the walls of separation. His one question is what his neighbors think of him. He peers over the walls and perceives evidence for his own detachment from danger. "Why," he exclaims, "they lie, cheat, steal, and commit adultery! Those people over there are sinners!"

He is correct. And as they peer over at him, their observations are also accurate. If one begins with man's sinful nature as the premise of all psychology, then we are in a fundamentally hopeless position, for sin has justified itself. But, as a matter of fact, sin has come as judgment upon sin, as we read in Romans 1 and in abundant experience. Man's love for sin as sin, without justification or rationalization, is the last (but rarely the first) step in the degrading descent.

Rather, the fundamental fact is that man has upon him the print of God's fingers. He is a sinner, but was created with the capacity for the divine nature. Every body-self is a potential temple for the breath of God. Every son of Adam can be spiritually reborn.

The breath of God was incarnate in a Man who was fully human. This breath was identified by His voice, His miracles, His actions, His death, and His resurrection, and is known to us as the "Spirit of life in Christ." The winds of God upon human life are not purposeless—they are of the Spirit. No one can manipulate the human spirit back into life. No beating of drums, no polished oratory, no highly-organized campaign can initiate the holy respiration back to life. This work is by the divine will, working through the divine counsel: "The wind blows where it wills, and you hear the sound of it, but you do not know whence it comes or whither it goes; so it is with every one who is born of the Spirit" (JOHN 3:8).

Christ commissioned the church to continue His ministry on earth by the power of the Holy Spirit: "Jesus said to them again, 'Peace be with you. As the Father has sent me, even so I send you.' And when he had said this, he breathed on them, and said to them, 'Receive the Holy Spirit" (JOHN 20:21,22).

The Spirit of God is at home with the spirit of all men. God is One; the spirit of man is one. The Spirit came and immediately bound into a unity of peace and purpose one people.

"And suddenly a sound came from heaven like the rush of a mighty wind, and it filled all the house where they were sitting. And there appeared to them tongues as of fire, distributed and resting on each one of them. And they were all filled with the Holy Spirit and began to speak in other tongues, as the Spirit gave them utterance" (ACTS 2:2–4). When the church was filled with the life of God, she could communicate to men in every condition, of every nature and nation. The breath of God was given to us by the Son of God, the Lord Jesus Christ: "Being therefore exalted at the right hand of God, and having received from the Father the promise of the Holy Spirit, he has poured out this which you see and hear" (ACTS 2:33).

The church now brings the Spirit of Christ to the world. Her task is not to make religious noises, inflate rolls, compile statistics, put clergymen into a political lobby, compete in the suburbs to see who can build the first with the most, play restaurant, produce vaudeville, run festivals, have dances, raise money, bake cookies, be snobbish, and act *respectable*—her task is to impart life and witness to its unity in the Lord of life, Christ Jesus.

I attended a church early one Sunday morning to bring a message to the graduates. Before the service, there was hearty breakfast, many peppy jokes, and lots of congratulations all around that the youngsters had "made it." I was asked if it wouldn't be nice of me to keep the message short, since there were a pile of dishes to clean before morning worship, and I agreed to be nice. I asked the pastor, "What's it all about? Why do you do it?"

He replied that they had done it for years, and the parents expected it. "Perhaps the youngsters need God's blessing for their future now that they are out of junior high. Maybe the parents like to have God approve their efforts in helping junior with his homework. The fellowship is good for us. Have another roll?"

The vehicle of the church has now too often become a dead weight. The world opens before us, requiring life and crying for it urgently. This means that the vehicle must abandon the glory of the flesh and give freely of the glory of the spirit. Its resources are an open mind, an open heart, a listening ear, the love of God, and the Word of the Spirit. The world must feel the kinship of the church breaking down the walls of separation, erected to safeguard our abominable fetishes.

The good and humble man of the Spirit is bathed in the light of all the heavens. He comes to life and welcomes it. Life is all around him and in him and in others. He is sent by Christ to men, and sees the worth in them, even when they fail to see it in themselves. The more he loves life, the more it speaks to him; and when people make their way to him, it is because they want to trust life as he is living it. There is no meaning to life without goodness and humility; therefore, the humble man trusts God and has faith in himself. He will be an apostle to sinners as Christ was, sent by His Father. He will be heard, because there is no pride in his apostleship. He trusts the truth no matter who verifies his trust, because his true self was created in the image of God and not in the image of imagination.

The mass intellectual and social movements of men tell us something about their spirit, either the dark or light side of their selves. There is truth for us in their search if we feel deeply the kinship. The truth has given us an instinct for the truth, and we can know what they seek when the winds of God are blowing over the dark and fetid decay of sin. We in Christ can honor their right to reach out.

For example, the leaders of the Negro revolution are sons of ministers, and one is a minister himself. They plan their demonstrations and move out from churches; but once outside, this revolution is not the institutional church on the march. Many churchmen will have nothing to do with it. In its momentum, it has gathered to itself many whose actions are plainly inimical to the Christian spirit.

Is the church, then, to be like a mother who huffishly sniffs at a child who has married in haste? The new family regrets that it received reluctant parental blessing, but it moves next door so that it might be close to the family. When it stands as an established and respectable home, there will no doubt be more cordial relations between mother and in-laws, and the father will invite them over often. The growing children know their ties, and, as the years go on, will broadcast afar the blessings of their heritage.

Can you hear the winds of God? Do you see His movements? Not always. But our hearts have been cleansed, and goodness beckons us, for it is the sound of His coming. The church is allied with goodness. Self-righteousness is an enemy, but since when has goodness and not sin been the enemy of the Gospel? Is it not hate, separation, suspicion, and panic which are our foes? When the church finds souls breathed on by God, seeking for the real glory, honor, and immortality through patient well-doing, are they far from eternal life, and does the church have no Life to convey? Must God forsake our neighbor when the Christian closes his heart?

The Christian standing as sentinel on the walls of the church may not know what is going on "down there." "Friend or foe?" he cries. How do they "down there" know? What will they answer? The Christian may take it upon himself as truth-bearer to answer for those outside. Certainly the Bible commands us to test the spirit of the antichrist and his idols. But there may be many "down there" who are friends in disguise and do not know it. We persist in answering for them.

"Recite me your creed," we shout down.

We have only two labels to paste on anyone's present perception, only two barrels in which to cast his understanding: right or wrong, truth or error. Failing to make a friend of pilgrims in their solutions that sound different from ours, we seek to bludgeon them out of their quest and talk them out of their own minds. When they will not listen, we decry the obstinacy of their pride.

In general, the people of the church do not consider loving to be the first order of business. It is dispensed with in a sermon or in an hour a month. A thousand people will bake and attend a festival, but not one will present the case for Jesus Christ over the back fence. Still, the church may take pride in its evangelism program, because ten elders and five deacons go out to sign up new members once a month. If they are poor salesmen, few prospects are signed up. If a family proves to be a poor prospect, no one returns: "They had their chance. Now they know the church doors are open." Very well. But the poor prospects are still ours—they are God's; the kinship remains. If the breath of God were upon us, we could have no other course than to love all who are prospects for eternal life. It is not for us to say where the winds of God will blow.

There is an "orthodox" side of the church, which is our anxiety. Its sons look with the distrust of their own spirit to the distrust of the spirits of men. In such perspective, the truth cannot be trusted to thrive in such barren ground as the human spirit, and must be shored up with the crutches of intellectual proofs and stored in the iron vaults of creeds. This seems natural if it be granted that the truth of life is the vault itself and that one is shaken with the impact of illumination if he subscribes to another's description of truth as it came to him. If the sinner permits his flagrant disregard of morality to show, then he has obviously defeated any attempt to live—he has fallen flat on his face, and that is as it should be. If, however, by some strange quirk, he leads a full and significant life for what is noble and lasting, then he becomes a serious problem, and is likely to be the object of all the creedal brickbats thrown at his head to give him a change of heart. But this is a battlefield he dearly loves, and one on which he rarely comes off second best. What shall we do with this man who is a problem because he is such a fine person? What is there to do but thank God for goodness! And then match him honor for honor, love for love, and give the glory to God. The winds of God will blow where they will. There are some who are closer to the Kingdom than they know, and our anxiety over the human spirit can serve only to drive them away.

If the world is not listening, it must be because the people do not feel the breath of God from our direction, or because when they do sense it, the church is convinced they are misled. Love speaks with no tongue and with all tongues. Love pays dearly for loving—love suffers. Paul said, "For this gospel I was appointed a preacher and apostle and teacher, and therefore I suffer as I do" (II TIMOTHY 1:11,12a).

If the world's goal is death through safety, ours must be life through death. The vehicle must die a thousand times a day in order that the Word of God may be unfettered. The Spirit honors His Word through love. To see a soul love life by putting himself out for another is a forceful argument—it is unanswerable. Faith is vindicated by love, and without love there is no vindication for there is no faith. No one can reasonably expect the world to mentally overcome barriers to belief which church people have not overcome in practice.

The philosophical rescue of the faith once delivered, a newer emphasis, shows no lesser anxiety. For it, the present glint of truth for any man or movement must be classified in its historical perspective and sifted through the creedal catalogs. We are told to study the writings of Prof. X and his followers. Our retreat is to libraries, not to the place where Prof. X lives. Traces of this thought bloc and that emphasis are traced down. Now we have a label for Prof. X. His stuff can safely be dismissed as post-Hegelian, pre-Freudian, neo-Bultmannism with traces of Bonhoeffer. Prof. X has been safely disposed of, because his words have been pickled, placed in jars, and stored in a showcase for inspection.

What then? Then the creedal conscience may be easier now in discussing The Issues with sophistication, but its rigid judgment from its own airtight system demonstrates little comprehension or sympathy with the heroic, searching spirit between the lines. Those who are cozy in a creedal vault are not inclined to recall that the truth was rashly windblown first in the stirrings of the human spirit. It is hard for any of us to sympathize with God's recklessness, or to recall that truth often steals into town somewhere in the dust clouds and street brawls of someone's overheated dissatisfaction. It is hard to believe that God would let His Spirit loose in just anybody. Many Christians do not believe that Jesus is able to take care of Himself.

The Pharisees did not think it too likely that God would let the Messiah be born in a cow shed, go to parties with racketeers, and die by a lynch mob. We get a little suspicious of goodness that doesn't have a name brand to identify it. As Charles Jefferson said, ". . . instead of weaving arguments by which to prove that apparent virtue must be something else, let us thank God for every evidence of His presence, no matter when or where the evidence is presented. Moreover, it is a hazardous thing to say that a man is not good because he does not fit into our program." The Episcopal prayer has a noble request: "Help us to place the truth above our conception of it, and joyfully to recognize the presence of the Holy Spirit wherever he may choose to dwell among men; through Jesus Christ our Lord. Amen."

It is true that the church specializes in truth. Truth, nevertheless, does its work of redemption when it is followed by the Spirit of life in Christ. It needs allies of open hearts before it can lead the church to where the action is, and God's power is ready: "Thus saith the Lord Jehovah unto these bones: Behold, I will cause breath to enter into you, and ye shall live" (EZEKIEL 37:5, *ASV*); "And I will put my Spirit in you, and ye shall live, and I will place you in your own land: and ye shall know that I, Jehovah, have spoken it and performed it, saith Jehovah" (EZEKIEL 37:14, *ASV*). With Ezekiel in mind, John spoke of God's witness being dead; then God intervened: "But after the three and a half days a breath of life from God entered them, and they stood up on their feet, and great fear fell on those who saw them" (REVELATION 11:11).

Breathe on me, Breath of God,
Fill me with life anew,
That I may love what Thou dost love,
And do what Thou wouldst do.

Breathe on me, Breath of God,
Till I am wholly Thine,
Till all this earthly part of me
Glows with Thy fire divine.

This must be the first and last test in our churches of every function, every device, every program, every venture: Is the breath of God upon it? For the church to spend effort in this world betrayed and twisted by sin, for her to spend an hour of precious time, preening her own feathers, staring at her reflection in her own mirrors, and polishing the ornaments of her own glory; this is idolatry so heinous that one can only sympathize with the people who stumble in their own way to find God's meanings for their existence. What does a dying man crave? He craves life. The church should not betray her own commission or misjudge her own importance. She brings nothing less than life. The church that studies the Word, and rises from prayer and enters the streets and homes to listen to the troubled, pray for the sick, feed the poor, witness to Christ, and encourage the weak, will be found where Christ was found, and will work the works of Christ and perhaps even greater works than those.

Consider the sermon as a means of bringing power from the life of God to the spirit of man. Here also we have a divinely appointed means of ushering souls into the sphere of hope, power, and truth. Redemption is on the wings of the sermon. Many illustrations of what we are saying could be employed, but the sermon is often the first formal contact of the church with a passing stranger.

Wherever we listen to the Protestant sermon on our family vacations, it can be seen readily that endless hours of preparation have gone into them. As a whole, the Protestant clergy is exceptionally well informed and shows keen perception of current issues. It is strange that so many of the sermons are boring, so many go completely over our heads. How can this be?

Unless the gift of preaching is a ". . . manifestation of the Spirit for the common good" (I CORINTHIANS 12:7), it will be a dialog with one's self. The sermon, with all its cleverness, can very easily be a contrivance to excite applause, with due reflection upon the preacher. It can be a shiny thing constructed out of interesting assorted bits of someone else's daring thoughts, scholarly research, denominational go-get-'em phrases, a dash of Scripture, and an excellent illustration going the rounds. Each phrase can be burnished and tightly fit into its exact place. And the people can audit the lecture and walk out into the cold world feeling cold. This comes as a surprise to the pastor who has spent hours over piles of books. "The age is secular," he laments.

Yes, secular. But nothing more secular than the sermon without flesh and blood, which acts as a mechanical device to call attention to the minister's secular fetish.

Yes, secular. The age is immersed in a sea of things, objects, places and hobbies held near to the heart.

Out of such things we can make our way back to the heart.

How? By (*1*) empathy, (*2*) assimilation, and (*3*) expression.

Consider *empathy*. This requires awareness of persons and a kinship of spirit. The pastor seeks not to superimpose his fetishes on others. He comes to them as spirits to be understood, felt after, known, and seen.

Empathy and understanding are what a good counselor feels when he listens with great attentiveness to a troubled person. It is what Jesus felt when He spoke to the woman of Samaria by the well. It is what a trusted friend feels when spirit opens to spirit. It is what Ezekiel felt when he was commissioned to bear a bitter message to his people: "The Spirit lifted me up and took me away, and I went in bitterness in the heat of my spirit, the hand of the Lord being strong upon me; and I came to the exiles at Telabib, who dwelt by the river Chebar. And I sat there overwhelmed among them seven days" (EZEKIEL 3:14,15). For seven long days he said little, but sat where they sat and felt what they felt. How can anyone speak to another without living from within the other's spirit for a time? The good message does not entertain—it brings Life to life, Spirit to spirit. The Spirit of life in Christ must form a bridge from soul to soul. One can preach on fetishes if he senses why persons use them, he can preach against sin if he feels the pains of the sinner; and these same sinners will listen while he speaks from the other end of the sanctuary if they feel he is close to their lives.

The closely allied process is *assimilation*. This is the weaving by our souls of fact and experience into a logically developed and emotionally forceful invitation to the full life God has for us in Christ. The mind and spirit are one in the holy person. Our spirits are related to all spirits by the creative Spirit of God. The Spirit can work in and through our minds to identify with persons and speak intimately to them.

Let me criticize by making what sounds like a ridiculous judgment—namely, that while thousands do not read, some of us *read too much!* The greatest instrument of creation outside of God's mind is our own mind, created in God's image. This mind needs time. It likes to have facts and observations and feelings placed into it. It likes to absorb the truth of the Bible. Then it does a miraculous work—it springs forth with an *urgent* and a *unique* declaration.

This is true for pastor and people. One church puts out a weekly paper called "Sermon Helps." It contains Scripture study for every day, based on the sermon of the coming Sunday. The subconscious absorbs these Scriptures and observations. Related experiences in everyday life add force to the processes of our spiritual computer. There is a unity to life because of God—matters tie together; insights come. Then there is the moment when we are able to arrive at the living, vital, shimmering, breathing thing—the God-breathed sermon. We feel it together. We understand each other. Experience is woven into a pattern. Life is precipitated for us to see and want it.

I'm not claiming for a moment that I do this either well or regularly, but I believe that this process should be explained. Recently my son Jamie brought some friends over, and on their way to his room they saw me staring out the window, assimilating.

"How come your father isn't out working?" one asked indignantly.

"His is working," replied Jamie.

"He is? What does he do for a living?"

Replied Jamie, with the characteristically gross exaggeration of a young fellow, "He thinks."

While there are many occupational hazards involved in not being too competent in the way we earn a living, nothing but rich rewards can accrue from sincerely attempting to live up to such a compliment.

The last means by which the minister can reach his congregation is *expression*. The clergy has been taught much about "audience contact"—that has been the problem. Groups of persons needing life have been treated as audiences. What good is a masquerade role without an audience? Audiences are chiefly required for audience-participation, acting out bit parts as part of the production, or showing approval or disapproval of the entertainment.

The preacher does not want an audience; he needs a partnership in the Gospel. As they have contributed to his spirit, so in this experience they know the breath of God's power through his passionate and sensitive declaration of the truth. His illustrations often come out of the raw materials of the pastoral kinship. He is excited about this venture into the fullness of life, and he calls earnestly as friend to friend. He pleads hopefully, "Come." His call is worded simply, directly, succinctly. The whole message is cohesively bound by a theme of certain concern. The implications may be daring, the art may be profound, but the whole should be crystal clear. The people must leave thinking, "God was with us and spoke to me. Now I must choose to answer, 'Indeed, Lord.' "

This kinship in the Gospel is not another role to disarm would-be opponents. While the spirit of evil is pacified by soft-soaping evil, souls go off stumbling, fumbling, bumbling. The truth spoken from a tender heart sears and burns human defenses. We sinners do not depart with a jolly disposition when our sacrosanct facade is burned like straw. Jesus made people angry enough to kill Him. But the Holy Spirit is the breath of truth, and unless a man is breathing this air, his life cannot be renewed. The good pastor has the best interests of his flock at heart.

Miracles are the stock in trade of the church. Whenever two or three or more persons meet in His name and in His Spirit, there is a circulation of power—love is breathed into the atmosphere, hope reigns. Out of our kinship, individuality thrives in freedom. The winds of God move on the human spirit as surely as the day when the Spirit of God brooded over the faceless earth. Exhausted by a world of frustrations, we are like runners in the race of life who gasp for air, and cry out for the breath of God.

We will live! His Spirit is with us still.

15

Swallowed Up by Life

AS THE NEW man with the Spirit of life in Christ yearns for the fullness of the richest possible life, he realizes he is encumbered by his own body. He senses more and more that he is in a body guaranteed to decay. Death is, as we know, part of man's judgment. Taking into account the fact of universal sin, man could not in the natural state—that is, in the space, time, mass condition—grow into perfect unity with God and the full realization of his unique humanity. Death-judgment takes into account his sin, and weighs in the balance his basic direction toward God or fetishes. Death-judgment serves the purpose of propelling man over the "unending" ages of space-time-mass into the terminal point of his direction—namely, heaven or hell. Man's life is brought to its completeness in the condition of eternity.

The sudden bridge over time to eternity is a gift of God's grace to the believer, who, with all his faults and faithlessness, is given the benefit of the doubt and the benefit of his faith. Judgment also satisfies the holiness of God, who justifies His faith in His children. This faith is based on His faith in Himself to bring to completion the creation destined for eternal and complete unity with Himself. God's witness to man includes the promise of eternal destination; therefore, both heaven and hell vindicate the sovereignty of God within the fact of man's limited freedom.

We like to think of our unique selfhood in terms of the "body." Some have talents, some are beautiful, some are clever, and some have superior athletic abilities. In the New Creation of God, however, distinctive contributions within the Kingdom of the Spirit are enabled through spiritual gifts. Sin has caused the body now to be the basis of our false sameness, our standard appearance, our cut-rate fetishes, our yoke within the mass mind. Full realization of ourselves is still before us, and obviously cannot be within the confines of this body of flesh and blood.

In his present stage of life man is required to live as flesh and blood. One assumption is that when man dies, his soul flies away somewhere like a bird, and that thereafter he must resemble Casper the Friendly Ghost frolicking freely on some playcloud. Well, that is good and weird. Mark Twain has already roasted us enough. Whatever man will be, we have got to begin with the fact that in this life the soul includes the body. God created man and he became an alive being, a human soul (GENESIS 2:7). He is a being of flesh and blood.

Man may distinguish mind from body, or use a hyphen (body-spirit) to becloud his own misunderstanding, but there is no hyphen—there is only *soul*. When one loves, or thinks, or hates, or prays, or hopes, every cell in his body is involved, right down to his toes, right up to the roots of his hair.

We think of "character" as a disembodied thing which rides on the body as a man rides on a horse. Character is the quality of life determined by decisions. These decisions are influenced by inherited temperament, the flow of the endocrine glands, the mood of the mind, the stirrings of the vestigial self, Jung's racial memories, the muscles, atmospheric conditions, cosmic rays, ions, nutrition, experience interpreted subconsciously, and by last evening's apple pie, to mention just a few. All these factors are, in turn, influenced by the supreme guidelines ingrained in the mind, those overall ideas about our roles, what we expect life to do for us, and the way we need people to treat us. All this is in the body, inscribed on the central and autonomic nervous systems, and stored in the tissues. Man is more than flesh and blood. But in this life he is certainly that at least.

This is the body with a mind of its own. It cannot depend on my poor thinking to plan the digestion of food, the breathing of air, the formation of babies, the repairing of tissues. It does this without my knowing precisely how. The body has set "ideas" of its own.

Thus, the body rules. Disregard its demands for long, and it threatens with death. And whatever high and mighty spiritual ideas we are going to fulfill, we'll not get them done in this life as corpses. First, see what the body wants.

When you are aliented from the unity of the Spirit of life, these persistent body ultimatums will clash, but they'll be attended to in time. And eventually we'll get around to forging a kind of microscopic unity, for all practical purposes, out of the bodily demands, because, after all, bodies have things in common—things you can count on. Selfish dominions are laid out, and tiny fleshly kingdoms rule in "safe" glory around the body and its extensions. By "extensions" we mean trinkets fitted to the body as part of the glory of the body, such as Dior gowns, new hairdos, very big diamonds, cosmetics, and Cadillacs. And greatly to be worshipped is the idea of a body disdaining supports and trappings, and openly standing on its two feet as glory personified, with just several inches of material to enhance the effect. Hail to the body, created by God wonderful, and renovated by man a stupendous object of adoration!

The body rules. It is to be identified with the person: "Show me his picture." And in the coffin dress him for his trip; see that wherever he lands in the afterlife, he looks presentable.

Microcosms reduce themselves to the glory of this world of the body. Pay to stuff the body. Diet! Work to grow it. Reshape it! Grow in debt to pamper it. Train it! Speed up time to make it look seventeen; hold back time to keep it at thirty. Break it down. Build hospitals to bring it back. Brace, stuff, remold, color, cut, and shape its parts to recreate the body in the image of the latest gods. Without the body? Heavens! Where would we be?

The anxiety over life and the anxiety over the body do the *Danse Macabre* together. Seven out of ten patients complain to the doctors of pains caused by anxiety. If the hand won't work, the whole person is guilty; if the voice box won't function, he's guilty here also. People are bodies. People-bodies break down when they are no longer whole. When they are sick, they are all sick. The sex gland becomes active, and the rest of the fellow goes along for the ride; the eyes fasten on the unwatched money, and the rest of him shares the conspiracy; he raises his voice in hate, but all of him stays awake nights. He is all of one organism!

The body is the temple of the First Creation. It is part of all the elements of all dust of the earth. As glorious as is the body, the burden of this and every other body in a world of sin and incompletion is terrible to be borne. We must suffer the burdens laid upon us by every living man. Nature can destroy the body—when a reservoir burst its dam in India, 1,000 bodies were destroyed. Someone carried germs to my neighbor's child, and she was sick for six weeks. Another child was deformed at birth, and doctors are mystified. We seem to be overwhelmingly crushed by the weight of Adamic sin infecting the weakness and futility of the body. The impulses to love, joy, courage, and the creation of beauty are stifled as a foot stamps out a small flame: "Wretched man that I am! Who will deliver me from this body of death?" (ROMANS 7:24).

It is God who brought the First Creation into being through Christ, who will bring to completion His New Creation through this same Christ. The New Creation begins with those in the body of death and is enveloped fully by the Spirit of God when a new body is created. Already the New Creation has come into being! "Therefore, if any one is in Christ, he is a new creation; the old has passed away, behold, the new has come" (II CORINTHIANS 5:17). Full unity with our God-created spirits, full entrance into the divine nature, and full participation with the Spirit of life in the work of God are possible only by the full realization of God's glory. Glory is restored the moment one faces the truth and receives the pardon and Spirit of Christ. "So with us; when we were children, we were slaves to the elemental spirits of the universe. But when the time had fully come, God sent forth his Son, born of woman, born under the law, to redeem those who were under the law, so that we might receive adoption as sons. And because you are sons, God has sent the Spirit of his Son into our hearts, crying, 'Abba! Father!' " (GALATIANS 4:3–7). Present justification and entrance into glory is a fact of the here and now (ROMANS 8:29,30). We are already raised with Christ! Christ is Lord of the Kingdom of which we are already a part! Already the flesh is being loosed by the Spirit in preparation for a new body like unto the glorious body of the Son of Man!

I remember a man by the name of Mr. Benton. He drove a taxi. Mr. Benton lived in a world all his own. It was confined to a route never consciously mapped out—up, eat, taxi, ride, eat, home, eat, TV, sleep, beer, sleep, up, eat. . . . He loved his wife and two daughters from a distance, and he proved his love by being *respectable*, turning over the money he earned, and staying out of trouble. He stayed out of everything else, including the church, and would no doubt boast, "I never did anything, Lord." It was impossible to speak to him of the larger actual life, because he was quite secure in the little world he constructed out of odds and ends. It was airtight; not even life was allowed to enter and rearrange things.

He underwent an operation. He was sure it was successful. Later his wife told him that he had cancer. He had had it for some time, but since he shut out all unpleasant matters, that was shut out, too. Then it was too late. He agreed to speak to the preacher, which to some people is the same as consenting to die.

Mr. Benton had an artificial smile. It was as if he pulled it out of a bag and wore it for a few moments as required, and then removed it for comfort. He sat on the large couch unsmiling as I spoke to him.

"What is left of life for me?" he asked.

"There is all of life, although, unless God works a miracle, you will not live it here as long as you were meant to. But there is life. The real life, still waiting for you."

He was stiff as a stick—unbending, unmoved.

In the hospital several weeks later, he waited for me to come and read the Bible. He seemed to wait for me to read Romans 8:9–11, where life is promised to our mortal bodies. Finally, he admitted that he wanted the Spirit of Christ to enter his body. Was it too late to receive Him?

"No," I replied, "it is not too late. God has kept you for this decision in behalf of life. He has been gracious to you."

On the last day, I was reading the Scriptures. I read again from Romans 8, and during the reading he took his leave. Just before he left, he smiled. It was a genuine smile, and I felt that he was on the verge of happiness.

His wife was terribly lonely. As we left the room, she said, "I guess our prayers were not answered."

I thought to myself, "My dear friend, that depends on what you were praying for."

Some of us were praying that Mr. Benton would exchange his papier-mâché glory for the glory of God. Mr. Benton's glory glittered like the thrills of a grade-D motion picture, was participated in by small robots, and was covered with dust and cobwebs. His was the glory of a man who whispers to himself in a dark corner, "You're getting by; what else is there?"

But something had happened to this man. God, who can be none other than the Sovereign Creator, resists what we so easily give ourselves to in order to usurp His power and glory. God reaches down, weakens, ages, threatens, and destroys flesh and blood. He strips away the body's fanciful extensions. Sickness and suffering are part of the price man pays to come within the freedom God actuates within our human condition, condemned in sin and burdened by racial pride. Man has created a world in which God cannot afford to hold inviolate the health of flesh and blood for the benefit of this tinsel glory. Flesh and blood will grow old. The world itself is under the sentence of time. To be born is to die. But before Mr. Benton passed on, he made a great discovery—it was revealed to him that his body-self was not exhausted by flesh and blood. No, he himself was far more than this. This life reborn in the New Creation was destined for something greater than he could imagine, and it was an order of being without decay.

"For this slight momentary affliction is preparing for us an eternal weight of glory beyond all comparison, because we look not to the things that are seen but to the things that are unseen; for the things that are seen are transient, but the things that are unseen are eternal" (II CORINTHIANS 4:17,18).

The sentence of death is on the First Creation. Death is birth. Suffering is permitted by God as birth pangs. Life is not realized without pain—all men suffer. To be born is to agonize. Augustine said that God had one son without sin, but not one without suffering. Terrible heartache, painful loneliness, torments of mind and body are the lot of Adam's sons. The Spirit comes as fire and wind to envelop with destruction the glory of the pride of man. Flesh and blood lose their power. The Spirit of life offers to be one with our spirits. The vessels of flesh are cracked and broken that the transcendent power of the true life may be revealed in all its glory. In the halls of the suffering, light shines. Reality shines as an angel of light. Alone is the life of God! Eternal! Glorious!

It is for this, our life, we cry out!

It is this life which quenches our thirst, feeds our hunger! The body of this flesh is the body which God has prepared for us now, but it shall be changed as we enter fully into the New Creation. The suffering saint cannot share the consternation of sympathizing onlookers. The Spirit-indwelt knows that ". . . the sufferings of this present time are not worth comparing with the glory that is to be revealed to us" (ROMANS 8:18). This suffering is a nostalgic holding hands with a passing creation of which we are so much a part. The saint no longer shares the same destiny, condemnation, futility, and loneliness of his fellows. It is, at the last, soley his sufferings which bind him to the old, even as through them he passes to the new. As a woman in great pain thinks only of the birth, so the saint destined for glory has a heart filled with anticipation.

My friend, Pastor Bill Gates of Cincinnati, told me of a soul who was once under his care. She lay in the nursing home, unable to speak. Her body was broken, ridden with pain, and paralyzed by many strokes. She fell out of bed and fractured her hip. Month after month she lay almost motionless. One afternoon shortly before she was taken by God, Bill visited her. He did the talking, of course, but before he left she strained every muscle within herself to speak. Bill said that it was by a miraculous and uncanny effort she got out three words: "God . . . is . . . good."

The Old Creation of flesh is fading. The New is coming into its own. Christ, the Herald of the New, has gone before us through suffering, redeeming our humanity, our very spirits. Christ Himself reveals the glory of God.

God's glory is the splendor of the complete and sublime life of the Creator, revealed in the full light of His truth and grace. It is all life in full unity with His holy omnipotence. It is beauty fully beautiful, truth in its majesty, goodness finished her work. We have hints of life. The breath of eternal glory is upon us. There are glints of the majesty on high, struck as sparks off the flint of time. We hunger for what is just beyond us, and we see it in the Christ who imparted those hungers to us in creation. Christ identifies what we were longing for. The glory of God is come. The joy is commitment to what might be complete. We do not now see what man could be in the full unity with the life of God, "but we see Jesus." By the grace of God, He tasted death for every man.

"For it was fitting that he, for whom and by whom all things exist, in bringing many sons to glory, should make the pioneer of their salvation perfect through suffering" (HEBREWS 2:10).

"Life" is the breath of God. The life of God became flesh, and came that we might have life abundantly. "And the Word became flesh and dwelt among us, full of grace and truth; we have beheld his glory, glory as of the only Son from the Father" (JOHN 1:14).

Life is now revealed in all its splendor in the light of truth and grace. Man has fallen short of the glory of God, but Representative Man, fully clothed in that glory, has come, and the Son of Man brings the eternal glory within the conditions of time.

"For it is the God who said, 'Let light shine out of darkness,' who has shone in our hearts to give the light of the knowledge of the glory of God in the face of Christ" (II CORINTHIANS 4:6).

Every second of time reminds us of the destiny for which we were prepared. Every weakness of the flesh reminds us that our new life is one with the Spirit of life in Christ. "All flesh is like grass and all its glory like the flower of grass . . ." (I PETER 1:24). What shall we conclude, then? "And after you have suffered a little while, the God of all grace, who has called you to his eternal glory in Christ, will himself restore, establish, and strengthen you. To him be the dominion for ever and ever. Amen" (I PETER 5:10,11). God is good. Amen.

In the New Creation through His power, breathes into man again the breath of His Spirit's life. The victory is to be alive to life in the Old as we are already passing to the New. We love life, but we are reconciled to the work of death. "For while we are still in this tent, we sigh with anxiety; not that we would be unclothed, but that we would be further clothed, so that what is mortal may be swallowed up by life. He who has prepared us for this very thing is God, who has given us the Spirit as a guarantee" (II CORINTHIANS 5:4,5).

This Spirit of life broods on the face of the Old and brings into being the New. "Now the Lord is the Spirit, and where the Spirit of the Lord is, there is freedom. And we all, with unveiled face, beholding the glory of the Lord, are being changed into his likeness from one degree of glory to another; for this comes from the Lord who is the Spirit (II CORINTHIANS 3:17,18).

Already the Spirit is transporting us and preparing us for the New. Already disillusionment has turned to repentance, and groping into faith. Already we have the firstfruits of life full-blown. Already the dayspring of glory has risen, and already we live in heavenly places with Christ. Already eternity draws us on. Already we are free from the stench of sin and decay, because the process of *metamorphosis* has begun. The Greek word "metamorphoo" means to change into another form. Christ was first *changed* ("transfigured"—the same Greek word) (MATTHEW 17:2). We are even now *being changed* by the life-giving Spirit (the same word) (II CORINTHIANS 3:18).

The ethical problem of bringing these earthly bodies into harmony with the Spirit—of actualizing in our body-selves our unity with the selfhood of Christ—is the task of growing whole in holiness. "I appeal to you therefore, brethren, by the mercies of God, to present your bodies as a living sacrifice, holy and acceptable to God, which is your spiritual worship. Do not be conformed to this world but be transformed by the renewal of your mind, that you may prove what is the will of God, what is good and acceptable and perfect" (ROMANS 12:1,2). Here the word "world" means age, the First Creation dominated by fetishes. The word "*transformed*" means to undergo metamorphosis—the same Greek word that characterizes our change for the New Creation.

Life which comes into its own has been prepared for those who have been prepared by God's Spirit. God chose bodies for the First Creation; we have not seen the glory of the vehicle God chose for the identity of our selves. Sin has mutilated the body, and death-judgment has come upon all, for all have sinned. In the New Creation, God has prepared new vehicles. The body of the First is soul—it is called a "soulish," or natural, body. This natural body was suited for the space-mass-time dimension of the First Creation. "It is sown a physical body, it is raised a spiritual body" (I CORINTHIANS 15:44). This new vehicle of identity of self is not of flesh and blood; it is curious that Christians cannot or will not accept this. They are certain that God will bring forth flesh and blood in the resurrection —they want the First Creation to be forever. They long to remain in the first dimension, although the Word states clearly, "I tell you this, brethren: flesh and blood cannot inherit the kingdom of God, nor does the perishable inherit the imperishable" (I CORINTHIANS 15:50). God chose one body. He will also choose another. How can one already have his life rooted in eternity and long for the everlastingness of time? On the face of it, this is impossible! If one believes that God, by His power to subject all things to His sovereign person, has brought the New Creation into being, why can he not believe that God has the power to prepare bodies suitable for the new order? The Word is clear: "But our commonwealth is in heaven, and from it we await a Savior, the Lord Jesus Christ, who will change our lowly body to be like his glorious body, by the power which enables him even to subject all things to himself" (PHILIPPIANS 3:20,21).

The wonder of the New Creation in eternity calls for more than imagination. We know that it will mean the complete realization of our lives; it will mean the full union with God's Spirit, without fluctuation, decay, darkness, or sin. The Spirit lets our imagination run wild, because it will be far more glorious than we could ever imagine. "But, as it is written,

> 'What no eye has seen, nor ear heard,
> nor the heart of man conceived,
> what God has prepared for those who love him,'

God has revealed to us through the Spirit. For the Spirit searches everything, even the depths of God" (I CORINTHIANS 2:9,10).

The matters of the New Creation are foreign to the modern

man, because the God of this power is unknown to Him. The Subject, Sovereign, and Center of this new order is God. To long for Him is to taste the rapture of the New. He must be All in All. He must be adored, and He alone. Yearn for Him and walk your first steps in the glories of eternity, for the Glory of the final world is God, the Everlasting One. We will rejoice in God, and our souls will exult in the One who has clothed us in the garments of salvation.

The newborn persons of God's final order will be a crown of beauty in His hand. They shall be His bride in Beulah land, and the bridegroom shall rejoice over them (ISAIAH 62:3–5). They shall be His people, and He will be with them forever.

If this be so, one ought to ask where the sentence of time is leading him: to the destruction of the First Creation? or to the glorious life of the New?

All the lights that have ever shone, all the sweet voices that have ever called, all the exquisite beauty which has caught our souls, are calling us to the vastness of life in God. We are all infants. Beyond us is a new day, new work, new ventures with God. This graduation is just the beginning. Death is not the end; it is the beginning. It is always beginning with God. From everlasting to everlasting, He is God. The end is temporary. The beginning is permanent. Stretching out forever beyond us is life.

Take my hand, and I shall take yours. Let us walk into our future together. Let us sing a hymn—a hymn for all to hear and join in singing: Thanks be to God! Thanks be to God! Hallelujah! For God gives us the victory through our Lord Jesus Christ.

than He, the God of life power is unknown to them. The [illegible] [illegible], and [illegible] of His new order [illegible] [illegible] [illegible] [illegible] of the New [illegible] He will [illegible] and He alone [illegible] Him [illegible] first steps in the [illegible] [illegible] the [illegible] would [illegible] the Everlasting God. We will [illegible] our souls will [illegible] the [illegible] [illegible] purposes in salvation.

[illegible] purpose of God's final order [illegible] a crown [illegible] His right. They shall be His and His [illegible], and [illegible] choice over them [illegible] They shall be His people, and He will be [illegible] one [illegible] where the [illegible] to the destruction of the [illegible] life of [illegible]

[illegible] the [illegible] [illegible] all the [illegible] that [illegible] called at the [illegible] can [illegible] of life in God [illegible] [illegible] beginning. It is always [illegible] God [illegible] to everlasting. [illegible] beginning is permanent. Everlasting the Forever [illegible] life.

[illegible] hand [illegible] [illegible] [illegible] [illegible] God [illegible] God [illegible] Jesus Christ.

Notes

PAGE	LINE	
13	2	Pierre Ceresole
13	24	Ralph Waldo Emerson
14	7	Abraham H. Maslow, *Religions, Values and Peak-Experiences* (Columbus, Ohio, Ohio State University Press, 1964).
15	7	Charles Hartshorne, *Reality as Social Process* (Boston, Mass., The Beacon Press, and Glencoe, Ill., The Free Press, 1953).
17	3	Francis W. Beare, *The Interpreter's Bible* (Nashville, Tenn., Abingdon Press, 1953), p. 168.
17	12	Anton T. Boisen, *The Exploration of the Inner World* (New York, Harper & Row, Publishers, Inc., 1936), p. 138.
17	17	*Ibid.*, p. 121.
17	31	Wayne Oates, *Christ and Selfhood* (Association Press, 1961).
17	33	Ludwig von Bertalanffy; see, for example, *Psychosomatic Medicine*, vol. xxvi, no. 1, 1964, an adopted address given at the 5th Conference on Psychiatric Research, Harvard Medical School, Cambridge, Mass., June 27–29, 1963.
17	38	E. Stanley Jones, *Abundant Living* (New York and Nashville, Tenn., Abingdon Press, 1942).
20	9	Henry Stack Sullivan
21	27	*Ibid.*
23	10	William Ernest Henley, "Invictus."
24	40	Donald Snygg and A. W. Combs, *Individual Behavior* (New York, Harper & Row, Publishers, Inc., 1948).
26	4	Eunice Tietjens, "A Plaint of Complexity," from

PAGE	LINE	
		Body and Raiment (N.Y., Alfred A. Knopf, Inc., 1919) pp. 13–16.
31	15	Dorothea Day, "My Captain."
36	32	*Time* magazine, vol. 87, no. 15, Apr. 15, 1966, p. 31.
36	39	Richard Adler, editor, in *Town Magazine*, London.
37	8	*Time* magazine, *op. cit.*, p. 33.
37	31	"The Anglican Community," *Time* magazine, Aug. 16, 1963, p. 60.
38	4	Rebecca West
38	23	Albert Einstein
38	28	Erich Fromm, "Our Way of Life Makes Us Miserable," in *The Saturday Evening Post*, July 25–Aug. 1, 1964, p. 10.
39	11	Erich Fromm, "Selfishness, Self-love, and Self-interest" (chap. v), in *The Self*, edited by Clark E. Moustakas (New York, Harper & Row, Publishers, Inc., 1956), p. 63.
40	32	Robert Louis Stevenson
40	34	*Westminster Catechism*
53	41	Floyd V. Filson, *Jesus Christ the Risen Lord* (New York, Abingdon Press, 1956), pp. 28, 29.
60	28	Kaijetan von Schlaggenberg
62	16	Sydney J. Harris, from column in *Akron Beacon Journal.*
65	10	Gregory Wilson, *The Stained Glass Jungle* (New York, Doubleday and Co., 1962), p. 80.
68	1	Martti Siirala, "Self-Creating in Therapy," in *The American Journal of Psychoanalysis,* vol. xxiii, no. 2, 1963, p. 171.
69	8	Francis W. Beare, *The Interpreter's Bible*, vol. 10 (Nashville, Tenn., Abingdon Press, 1953), p. 628.
71	5	Charlotte Elliott, "Just As I Am," 1836.
73	3	Reul Howe, *The Creative Years.*
77	19	Ralph Spaulding Cushman, "Thank God I'm Alive," from *Hilltop Verses and Prayers* (New York and Nashville, Tenn., Abingdon Press, 1945).
78	8	Allen Gardiner, *diary.*
78	23	Adelaide Anne Proctor, "My God I Thank Thee," 1858.
79	6	C. Moore Hunt, "Word from the Prodigal," in *The*

PAGE	LINE	
		Christian Century, vol. LXXXI, no. 27, July 1, 1964, p. 854.
83	2	James Michener
84	12	Gene Fowler quotes W. C. Fields.
91	20	William James
91	35	Van Wyck Brooks
92	1	Montaigne
92	34	J. S. Mill
93	11	John Kord Lagemann, "Forgiveness: The Saving Grace," in *Christian Herald*, Jan., 1961.
97	1	Ann Landers column, in *Akron Beacon Journal*, Aug. 22, 1964.
97	27	Oscar Wilde
99	12	"If You Believed in Me"
101	32	Joseph Mary Plunkett, "I See His Blood Upon the Rose," in *The Collected Poems of Joseph Mary Plunkett* (Dublin, Talbot Press Ltd.).
104	35	Ralph Waldo Emerson
105	22	Fiorello H. LaGuardia
105	36	Arturo Toscanini
107	11	John Greenleaf Whittier "O Lord and Master of Us All."
108	4	Oscar Eliason, "Got Any Rivers."
111	39	Jim Whittaker
112	15	I. A. R. Wylie, in *Reader's Digest*, Mar., 1953, and June, 1963.
113	22	Adam Lindsay Gordon, "Ye Weary Wayfarer. Finis Exoptatus."
113	34	Eric Liddell
116	24	Ogden Nash, "Kind of an Ode to Duty," in *Verses from 1929 On* (Boston, Little, Brown and Co., 1959).
118	4	"Eichmann and the Duty of Man," *Life* magazine editorial.
118	40	Ralph Waldo Emerson
120	31	Martin Niemöller
122	17	Isak Dinesen
122	36	William Wordsworth, "Ode to Duty."
126	15	Dr. O. F. Rosenow
126	28	W. G. Carleton
126	38	I. A. R. Wylie

Page	Line	
127	26	Henry Thoreau
128	1	Alan B. Shepard, Jr.
129	40	Erasmus
130	10	Gustave Flaubert
133	14	Leo Tolstoy
134	7	Samuel Johnson
134	12	Lord Rootes
135	33	Florence Nightingale
136	3	Dr. Samuel Gridley Howe
136	26	Henry Cabot Lodge, Jr.
137	26	Powell Buxton
138	34	Florence Nightingale
139	1	Thomas A. Edison
139	24	George Bernard Shaw
140	14	Abraham Lincoln
141	3	John Hay
141	7	Phillips Brooks
141	39	Dorothy L. Sayers
143	17	Betty Friedan, "Woman: the Fourth Dimension," in *Ladies' Home Journal*, vol. LXXXI, no. 5, June, 1964, pp. 48, 49.
144	20	Max Ehrmann, "A Prayer," in *The Best Loved Poems of the American People*, edited by Hazel Felleman (New York, Doubleday & Co., Inc., 1936), pp. 306, 307.
146	19	T. S. Eliot, *The Cocktail Party*.
148	2	Advertisement of Memorial Park.
149	25	Nicholas Berdyaev
150	30	Ernest Gordon, *Through the Valley of the Kwai* (New York, Harper & Row, Publishers, Inc., 1962).
152	10	Catherine Marshall
152	15	Dean Walter Robert Matthews
153	38	Arabella Catherine Hankey, "Tell Me the Old, Old Story," 1866.
154	31	Lona Fowler, "A Great Thought," in *Concern*, Feb., 1964.
165	38	Charles Jefferson
166	21	Edwin Hatch, hymn.
176	38	Augustine